TALKING SHANKLY

TALKING SHANKLY

THE MAN, THE GENIUS, THE LEGEND

TOM DARBY

MAINSTREAM
PUBLISHING

EDINBURGH AND LONDON

Copyright © Tom Darby, 1998

First published in Great Britain in 1998 by
MAINSTREAM PUBLISHING COMPANY (EDINBURGH) LTD
7 Albany Street
Edinburgh EH1 3UG

This edition 2001
Reprinted 2005

ISBN 1 84018 493 0

A catalogue record for this book is available from the British Library

Typeset in Sabon
Printed and bound in Great Britain by Antony Rowe Ltd, Chippenham, Wiltshire

For Tommy Cleland, a good man, and for Heather, Christine, Megan and Dylan, my children and grandchildren for whom I walk on through the storm with hope in my heart.

Contents

Foreword

By Emlyn Hughes

SHANKS

Just saying his name sounds special. I was fortunate to know Shanks for 16 years and I can only say, without shame, that I loved him. For Mrs Shankly to say that I was closer to him than anyone is the greatest trophy I ever lifted. Funny, witty, serious, hard but always human, the man could light up any room. When my father died, Shanks came to the funeral and back at mum's house afterwards, he had everyone there standing to attention telling stories about my dad.

Sat in Shank's front room with Ness serving us tea and biscuits, Bill said, 'Em, son, I'm going to tell you the real reason I left Liverpool . . . ' A knock at the door, it was his daughter with the grandchildren, and I will never know why he left Liverpool.

Boss, we all loved you.

Emlyn.

Shanks for the Memories

A few words of introduction from some of the all-time greats:

'Tom Darby's new book about Bill is a most welcome addition to the many past tributes which have been paid to my old footballing colleague and very closest friend, Bill Shankly.

Bill was indeed a legend within his own lifetime. His contribution both as a player for club and country, and team manager at various clubs was immense. A man whose proud Scottish Lion Heart knew no compromise both on and off the field, Bill dedicated his life to the 'People's Game' and its supporters. I remember Bill with pride and affection in his various capacities at Preston North End and with the greatest admiration for his achievements at his beloved Liverpool FC.

Ayrshire and Scotland can be rightly proud of Shankly, a man who is remembered fondly at Proud Preston. It's fitting that this addition to the Shankly lore keeps his memory alive into the new millennium so many years after Bill's passing. It was a privilege to have known and worked with the man and to have added this little contribution.'

Tom Finney

* * * * *

'I'm delighted that Tom's book gives us the chance, once again, to remember Bill – the man who was such a messiah, who gave Liverpudlians the courage and conviction to walk through the shadows of hard times. Bill provided the beacon which carried Liverpool FC from the obscurity of second division football towards what the club is today.

I'm thankful that I met Bill Shankly who gave a skinny Scouse kid, whom he said was 'tossed up with a sparrow for its legs and lost', the chance to become a pro footballer. Bill had faith in me and so many like me who, once under his wing, could do nothing else but succeed in the game our mentor was himself so passionate about.

Shankly was the 'people's man', a great spirit who created a family at Liverpool FC. LFC was the 'people's team' where fans and players were one unit with one common goal – to let the world know that Merseyside was alive and kicking and would, through our togetherness, succeed at the highest levels.

I was one of seven kids who was, along with our mam, a dyed-in-the-wool redneck. I loved Liverpool FC as a lad and am eternally grateful to Shankly for giving me the opportunity to play for my club in front of my own people, who are the finest on earth.

I miss Bill dearly but welcome the chance, through this publication, to browse over Bill's life and content myself with the fact that I once worked under, and lived beside, one of the greatest men that ever lived.

He took us to the promised land! For that, he lives forever on Merseyside.'

Phil Thomson

* * * * *

'It is with the greatest of pleasure that I contribute a few words of introduction to Tom Darby's new book about my former manager and mentor, Bill Shankly.

Shanks was an immense man whose passion and commitment to 'The People's Game' and those whom it served to entertain, were unrivalled in his time. A people's man in the true sense of the word, Shanks gave Liverpool much more than great teams and blueprint for the new Anfield coaching and stadium facilities – he gave Liverpudlians a pride in their city and a beacon to follow in a time of great economic decline on the Mersey shores.

I was indeed proud to have served as part of Shankly's 'Red Army'. You can erect gates and statues to Bill by the dozen, but the real tribute to this man is the fondness and high regard held for him in the hearts of Merseysiders, Ayrshire folk and all who came in contact with – the Legend, the Genius, the Man.

To me, Anfield will always be known as 'The Shankly Stadium' – perhaps we should rename it!'

Kevin Keegan

1

It Started in Glenbuck

Glenbuck village, now a few ruined stones scattered on the Ayrshire moors three miles from Muirkirk, nestles by the roadside in a tract of undulating countryside. The now uninhabited mining hamlet, soon to be transformed into yet another Scottish opencast coal-mining site, was the destination of a pilgrimage in March 1997 when several hundred supporters of Liverpool FC congregated to pay homage to Glenbuck's most famous son.

They arrived in coachloads to dedicate a black granite plinth, symbolising the shining Ayrshire coal, inscribed with gold lettering. They listened to tributes paid to Shankly by former villagers, ex-footballers and the great man's family. They sang 'Amazing Grace', Shankly's favourite hymn and shed tears as they joined hands, singing the anthem of Liverpool FC, 'You'll Never Walk Alone'.

A special guest on that occasion was Jack Moran, a 67-year-old Scouser from Endbutt Lane, Crosby, who walked the 230 miles from Liverpool's home at Anfield for St Joseph's Cancer Sanatorium in Shankly's adopted city.

They shed tears, they remembered with pride, Shankly's achievements as manager of their club and, imitating past Wembley Scots, took turf from Glenbuck back to their gardens in Bootle, Wallasey, Anfield, The Dingle and Tue-brook before the opencast bulldozers moved in.

They rejoiced on hearing from Scottish Coal that their Shankly memorial plinth would be returned to a special Shankly Garden on the former Glenbuck village site on cessation of opencast operations and landscaping of the moorland by the new millennium. 'We'll come back in our thousands to re-dedicate that site,' said Liverpool FC Away Supporters Club chairman Jimmy Flowers. 'This little part of Scotland is ours and lives in the hearts of all Scousers.'

Another Red quipped: 'There's a lot of kids at school in Liverpool who maybe don't know where Albania is but, by God, they all know Glenbuck!'

Never in all the history of British football has there been a village such as Glenbuck.

Back in the 1800s, Glenbuck village was born when, firstly, agriculture, weaving and lead-mining industries were in operation. Then, as demand grew for high quality Ayrshire coal to supply west of Scotland iron foundries, 'King Coal' gave prosperity to south Ayrshire.

The coal pits provided employment for Glenbuck villagers who drew together as a small tightly-knit mining community. Glenbuck's population up to the outbreak of the First World War is reported to have reached around 1,200 souls living close to their workplaces in the mines or on the land in neat little houses each with its own garden and vegetable plot.

The toil of village men was arduous as the early exploitation of coal and ironstone grew in the early nineteenth century. Mine owners spent little on the health and safety conditions of their employees who laboured long and weary hours, returning home to wash after a shift, in the decades prior to the advent of pithead baths. Mine accidents and fatalities occurred regularly. These conditions, though, generated a camaraderie, a close-knit dependence upon one another amongst neighbours in mining villages such as Glenbuck.

Working together in the bowels of the earth, each man depended on his workmates. Mineworkers were a 'family';

indeed, brothers, fathers, cousins and sons laboured alongside each other – one looking out for the other as the back-breaking work carried out in extremely dangerous conditions provided succour for their families.

In the days prior to insurance or compensation payments, or when these amounted to a pittance, neighbours would rally to provide for a wanting family.

The early socialism of Keir Hardie received its spark from these hard-toiling, close communities whose strength came from their unity and their solidarity. The kirk, too, played its part in Glenbuck as many villagers sought comfort, relief and guidance from the pulpit. Villagers had, in 1882, raised the enormous sum of £2,000 to build and stipend their own kirk. Glenbuck was a hard, isolated mining village where winters were long, but it is recalled by former residents as 'a happy wee place' where men worked hard and where women 'gave brightness and beauty'.

Glenbuck women were fiercely house proud, self-sufficient and dextrous in matters of cooking, sewing, altering clothes, and were 'guid mothers'. Robert Burns's humility and understanding of folk's faults and foibles is shown in his 'Address to the Unco Guid':

Then gently scan your brother Man,
Still gentler sister Woman;
Tho' they may gang a kennin wrang,
To step aside is human.

His many works extolling the value of honest work and the greater value of honest working people were embodied in Glenbuck village life where, as long as you pulled your weight, did no harm to your fellow villager, you were all right. Gossips, those of a jealous disposition, workshys or egotists were frowned upon and, on several occasions, banished from a community which many decades later gave birth to a philosophy in politics which was to carry Glenbuck's most famous former resident to glory both on and off the soccer pitch.

It was into this social milieu that on 2 September 1913 William Shankly was born. The youngest of John and Barbara Shankly's five sons and five daughters, the Shankly babe arrived at a time when, due to the outworking of nearby pits where lack of investment made top-grade coal hard to reach, Glenbuck's population had decreased to around 600 people. Men were leaving in droves to seek work in other similar coal villages or gravitating into the towns of Ayr and Kilmarnock for alternative employment.

Young Willie, as he was always known by family members, was born, as were his siblings before him, in his parents' bed in Auchenstilloch cottages, an area of Glenbuck known as Miners Row or 'Monkey Row'. Due to the size of the Shankly family, two 'Monkey Row' cottages had been converted to provide one family home.

Life wasn't easy for John and Barbara Shankly. With themselves and ten children to account for, they certainly struggled and had to dig deep into their resourceful characters to raise their brood. John Shankly was a tailor by trade, moving into Glenbuck towards the end of the last century where stints as a postman and tailor provided income for his family. An honest, forthright man, John was renowned throughout Ayrshire and south-west Scotland for his superb athleticism. A runner, Shankly Sr was a strict teetotaller and non-smoker. Later in life, Bill Shankly recalled his father as being '100 per cent honest', a stickler for high standards of behaviour, 'strong on self-discipline and plainly not an aggressive man, one who demanded, and got, the respect of his peers and family'. A highly principled man, John Shankly knew his Bible and commanded his sons to abide by the maxims of honest and clean living. Shankly remembered his father's 'unquenchable spirit' for life 'which I luckily inherited'.

As a good middle-distance runner, John Shankly scored a memorable half-mile win over celebrated Scottish runner Canty Young in the 1890s and introduced into Glenbuck fitness training classes. Powerfully built, he encouraged those around him to take care of their bodies, adopt standards of discipline and fitness to carry them through their lives, while at the same time, through his tailoring services, insisted that those around him 'turn themselves out well' in their attire.

This early in Shankly's life, we can see the lasting impression his father had on his son's development.

It was Willie's mother Barbara, however, who kept the family together during the tough times. A member of the celebrated Blyth family of Glenbuck, it was Barbara who passed on down the line the footballing abilities inherited by her sons. Her brother Bob – nicknamed 'Reindeer' due to his sprinting abilities – played senior soccer with Glasgow Rangers, Middlesbrough, Preston and Dundee, finally ending his career as player-manager then director at Portsmouth FC.

Another brother, William, also plied his footballing skills at Portsmouth and Preston before becoming a director then chairman of Carlisle FC.

Shankly recalled Barbara as being a 'wonderful mother' and in later life heaped tribute upon tribute on her ability to make ends meet with only a tailor's meagre wage whilst keeping the family home spotless, ensuring her children were well fed and immaculately turned out.

Although he kept an abstemious household, John Shankly was known to stray. A bottle of whisky was kept on the shelf at Monkey Row and on ten occasions, at the birth of each of his children, a dram was taken, in good Scots tradition, to welcome the latest arrival.

Schooldays for Willie were indeed 'learning days'. As he grew he witnessed the hardship endured by fellow villagers which held a lasting impression upon him. His five sisters – Netta, Elizabeth, Isobel, Barbara and Jean – would take their turns helping mother around the house, washing clothes by hand at the village household until, as with thousands of other working-class Scots lasses, domestic service to the well-off beckoned.

Barbara Shankly's sons, however, had an escape route from a life of hardship and eventual unemployment in the fast economically declining Glenbuck.

Football, both for them and for many of Scotland's mining

sons, was their passport to a better life. What made Glenbuck so remarkable in the annals of Scottish, and British, football was that the village produced, from such a small population, an inordinately high percentage of village men who went on to achieve on the soccer pitch.

With no public transport serving Glenbuck, no cars or motor-bikes, village men turned to their own community to create their entertainment. Hill running, quoits, John Shankly keep-fit classes, moor walking and hard work combined to create generations of fit young athletes who, in the days before TV and radio, soon found hours of pleasure kicking footballs around. The local junior football team, 'The Cherrypickers', was so named following an incident when, as legend has it, men from Glenbuck and Muirkirk, serving with the 11th Hussars during the Peninsular War in Spain, arrived at a Spanish cherry orchard and raised the fruit.

Another story has men from Glenbuck serving with the Hussars, who wore cherry red breeches, during the Boer War. No matter the origin of their name, the Glenbuck Cherrypickers won many honours, including the Ayrshire Junior Cup in 1889, '90 and '91. In 1906 they won the Ayrshire Charity Cup, Cumnock Cup and Mauchline Cup. The Ayrshire Charity Cup was again won in 1910 and the Cumnock Cup in 1901, 1903, 1904, 1905 and 1921. In their final years the Cherrypickers in 1931 lifted the Ayrshire Junior Cup. But the real place of Glenbuck is in its history as a nursery of famous footballers. Over 50 Glenbuck sons played senior football in Scotland, Northern Ireland, England and the US. Teams such as Kilmarnock, Ayr United, Hearts, Celtic, Rangers, Newcastle United, Blackburn Rovers, Tottenham Hotspur, Preston North End, Liverpool and Dundee headed a host of clubs who recruited from the skilful Cherrypickers sides.

No less than seven village men who entered professional football were capped to play for Scotland:

William Muir versus Ireland 1907
Alec Brown versus England 1902, 1904

George Halley versus England 1910
John Crosbie versus Wales 1920; versus England 1922
Bob Shankly versus Ireland 1938

The most capped villager, however, was Willie Shankly, being honoured 13 times between 1938 and 1943 (five full and eight wartime internationals).

Alec McConnell was selected to play against England but signed for Everton two days before the match, thus becoming ineligible, in those days, as an Anglo-Scot.

Other Cherrypickers gained international recognition at Junior level. It was upon these glorious village footballing foundations that Shankly and his brothers, Alec, James, John Jr and Bob, spent their formative years. It was these foundations which would give them a firm footing on their respective roads towards celebrated careers in football. And it was with other village lads that Shankly, on leaving school with the most basic education, entered the mines in 1927. Being 'broken in' to pit work, he first worked at 14 years of age on the pithead separating coal from stones, or redd as it was called. Following a six-month initiation, he went underground leading coal tubs onto the pit cage, then delivering 'empties' back to the mine's faceworkers for loading.

Shankly's education for life developed during these early teen years. Although conditions underground were coarse, he enjoyed working with the proud mining men. Memories were still strong of the mine workers' struggles of the 1920s and the May 1926 General Strike when, due to the lack of investment by mine owners and a currency crisis, the coal industry was in recession. The owners' solution was pit closures, longer hours and pay cuts. Following the '26 strike, the miners, striking alone for seven months and abandoned by Labour MPs, were starved back to work in deplorable conditions. Colliery after colliery closed. The young Shankly eyed these courageous men whose hard toil and discipline, family and community values he admired. These were his people; a proud, honest people, struggling to keep their families' heads above water – yet they were being attacked by the Conservatives, betrayed by their own Labour representatives in Parliament and exploited by owners and chairmen of mine-owning companies. The seeds of hatred for an exploiting, moneyed class, mistrust of MPs, and a belief that the 'workers' should have nothing but the best had been sown. Socialism had arrived into Shankly's heart.

Unemployment followed quickly. Following a short two-year mining 'career', Shankly was declared redundant as the last coal was mined in Glenbuck. Another career, however, was just around the corner.

To help family finances during a time of depression, the young redundant collier took on a paper round but football was fast becoming his first love. Although recognised locally as an aspiring soccer talent, Shankly was, at 16, too young to sign for the great Cherrypickers. He was a regular at training sessions, but by the time he was old enough the great club had disintegrated. Nearby Cronberry Juniors, however, liked what they saw in Shankly and signed the lad as a replacement right half-back.

This position at Cronberry soon became Shankly's property. At 19 he was surviving the hard school of Scottish Junior football and in true Glenbuck tradition, 'shone above the rest'.

The Shankly boys were beginning to make their illustrious marks on the great game. Willie was destined to join the professional ranks south of the border, whilst his brothers before him had soared in their careers.

Alec, eldest of the brothers and 20 years older than Willie, had played with Ayr United and Clyde before retiring from the game. Next eldest brother, Jimmy, displayed his ball skills at Carlisle, Sheffield United and Southend before moving on to Barrow, where he accomplished an all-time club scoring record of 39 goals in one season before returning to Carlisle.

Middle brother John turned out for Portsmouth, Luton Town, Halifax, Coventry City and Alloa Athletic. Bob Shankly, a few years older than Willie, spent 17 years at Falkirk, winning promotion to the Scottish First Division and gaining a Scottish League cap against the Irish League in Belfast. Following his footballing days at Falkirk, Bob had a successful career as manager of that club, as well as Dundee and Hibernian in Edinburgh before ending his football association as general manager and director of Stirling Albion.

Willie never forgot that, as his older brothers pursued their footballing careers, money was always sent to augment a poor family income.

One sad reflection on the lives of the Shankly brothers, though, is that in 1960 brother John collapsed in the stand at Hampden Park during the Real Madrid versus Eintracht European Cup final. He died later that evening at Glasgow's Victoria Infirmary. (The author remembers the occasion when, attending the match as a schoolboy, the buzz could be heard in the enclosure – 'one of the Shanklys has taken ill'.)

Whilst turning in polished displays at Cronberry, Shankly was spotted by a Carlisle United scout who recommended him to Bill Blyth, Carlisle director and young Willie's uncle, who wasted no time in inviting the promising young all-action half-back to Brunton Park, Carlisle, for trials.

2

Joining the Pro Ranks

The young Shankly had not strayed far from his Ayrshire moors. Previous ventures had been restricted to the odd visit to Glasgow, when funds allowed, to see either Rangers at Ibrox or Celtic at Parkhead. On his first trip out of Scotland, Willie was accompanied by his brother Alec and, as he remembered later, 'I felt so important as I walked through the club's gates'. He was obviously relieved and overjoyed that, like his brothers before him, he had escaped the poverty of unemployment in a fast declining south Ayrshire coalfield.

He was free! Free to embark upon a journey which would take him to unimaginable heights.

On entering Carlisle station, though, his thoughts would have returned to those great people, worthy men and caring women, whose honesty, dignity and determination to overcome adversity left its mark upon him. He would have remembered those who cheered on from the touchlines at junior matches or the thousands who thronged to Ibrox or Parkhead using the vehicle of an afternoon's football as their escape from their hard, ill-rewarded toil. Schoolbook learning did not, perhaps, amount to much in young Willie Shankly's life, but the knowledge gained through life with 'his ain folk' was already shaping this youth's character and would add to the development of his own charisma.

Wages at Carlisle were generous. Shankly signed on for a fee of £4 a week, rising to £4 10s on entry into the first team. Princely sums indeed compared to 2s 6d a day earned back home.

Mother had nevertheless warned that these wages may seem big, but that rent, light, heating, clothing and food would all have to be paid for. Although Bill was eager to send a proportion of his new-found wealth home, she steadfastly refused the offer. Now her family was up and running, she needed little. 'If I have enough, I have plenty and want no more.'

Carlisle were a club continuously struggling to make ends meet. Only around 30 years old when Shankly joined, they had gained entry into the Third Division North in 1928–29 and found weekly expenses and running costs a nightmare. Under increasing financial pressure, Carlisle brought in a host of young, promising juniors whom they hoped to groom alongside a few hardened but ageing pros.

Shankly roomed in Carlisle with a seasoned campaigner in the lower English leagues, club full-back Bob Bradley and fellow Scot Johnny Kelly, the club's goalkeeper.

He soon settled to life in the northern railway town. Carlisle's trainer, Tommy Curry, took to the young Shankly immediately. Following a trial match on 20 August and an outing in a reserve match against Middlesbrough reserves on 27 August 1932, the young Scot was offered a full-time contract at Brunton Park.

Curry had played alongside Shankly in the trial match, quickly forming an opinion that this lad's skill and high standard of fitness would carry him through reserve football and into the first eleven in a short period of time.

Becoming a father figure to the youngster, Curry encouraged Shankly in training and helped him build a confidence in his abilities which would propel him into first-team selection. Shankly had learned another lesson in life: those who encourage youth, those who care about the well-being and development of young footballers, will gain the gratitude and respect of those youngsters trying to break through.

Curry's contribution to the development of youngsters at Carlisle was soon noticed by Matt Busby who encouraged the trainer to join Manchester United's coaching staff. Later, Shankly was deeply upset on hearing Curry had perished in the Munich air disaster.

A regular in Carlisle reserves during 1932, young Shankly shone in the right-half position. Just after Christmas of that year he made his first-team debut, a league game against Rochdale which was drawn 2–2.

Sixteen first-team appearances followed during that season, at the end of which Carlisle finished in nineteenth position, narrowly escaping having to seek re-election to the league. At the close of the 1932–33 season, young Shankly returned home to spend summer with his family in Glenbuck. Shankly later recalled his thoughts travelling north for the summer break: 'For as long as I can remember my sole aim in life was to play football. When I worked down the pit all I dreamed about was the end of the shift and legging it to the nearest field for a game.'

Indeed, as he re-entered Glenbuck his thoughts returned to those daily 11-a-side matches with his workmates, 'tournaments' which were cut down to five-a-side games during summer months. Now he was a professional man being paid for playing the game, free from financial worry, plying his new trade which was nothing compared to the toil of a miner.

Back home amongst his 'ain folk' Shankly continued training. Road-running, ball practice and quickly arranged kick-abouts with the village lads kept him occupied until, he thought, his return to Brunton Park.

Preston North End had been keeping an eye on Carlisle's promising Ayrshireman and had previously made a move for him. Determined to land the right-half, the Deepdale club had offered cash-strapped Carlisle £500 for Shankly's transfer. Carlisle were having a clear-out of players and manager Billy

Hampson, for whom Shankly had the greatest respect, was moving on. As news of these changes reached Glenbuck, young Shankly became somewhat upset – he had settled in at Brunton Park and had come to feel at home with team-mates who were now moving on. However, as he pondered these changes, Shankly received a surprise when a telegram arrived in Glenbuck reading: 'Report Carlisle to discuss transfer to Preston North End.'

Shankly was over the moon at this communication. Preston were a big club. If they seriously required his services then he must be doing the right things. A fitting reward, he felt, for a hard season's work in which he played to the best of his ability.

On the day following the telegram's arrival, Willie was once more accompanied over the border by his brother Alec. On the journey south by train, Shankly shared with his brother his mixed emotions. On one hand he had become a first-team regular at Carlisle, albeit in a lower division, but on the other, he would have to return to reserve team status at Deepdale. Whilst Preston reserves played to a higher standard than Carlisle's first eleven, he felt he was learning his trade at Brunton Park. Preston had struggled in the Second Division; who was to say that another poor season might not see them joining Carlisle in the lower league?

Willie and Alec arrived at their Uncle Bill Blyth's bowling green pub in Carlisle where the meeting involving the young Scot and representatives of Carlisle and Preston was scheduled to take place. Preston's man was trainer Bill Scott who, following introductions, negotiated in private with Shankly.

Carlisle were keen to receive the £500 transfer fee previously agreed by both clubs, whilst Scott demonstrated an air of confidence that the youngster would have no hesitation in joining the bigger outfit. A signing-on fee of £40 was discussed and Scott informed Shankly that his present weekly wage of £4 10s would increase by ten shillings to £5.

Now the country lad faced a dilemma. Was Preston not a large city where a young man would find great difficulty in securing digs at the 25 shillings he was paying in Carlisle? He would have to pay money for his keep in such a metropolis as Preston.

Besides, he was at home in Carlisle, surrounded by friends and enjoying fame and adulation as a star in the town's team. On reflection, this move did not really seem all that great. His own, and others', redundancy in the coalfields had left its mark. What if he failed at Preston? Was it back to the village, shamed and jobless? Naïvety and uncertainty were manifesting themselves blatantly as Shankly struggled through the meeting with Scott.

Preston were big, but the young Shankly had memories of the 'big people'. Mine owners and politicians had exploited and betrayed his people. Robert Burns's dislike of the smart, moneyed, big city folk reared its head. Loyalty to the supporters of Carlisle was a consideration and, after all, wasn't he in the business of playing football to please himself and entertain those hard-working fans who sought release through the weekly matches at Brunton Park?

It wasn't about money, he pondered, it was all about playing the game and remaining loyal to those who had given him his opportunities and encouraged him.

He had a 'good job' at Carlisle, Preston was an unknown quantity. At first, Shankly turned Preston down. He was happy where he was, so much so that a ten-shilling-a-week rise wasn't enough of an incentive for him to move. More than a little disappointed, Bill Scott left to catch the afternoon's south-bound train.

On Scott's departure, Alec, hearing of his brother's decision, exploded with rage. Willie had given up the opportunity of playing for a long-established, respected and well-supported club. Alec was convinced the youngster had the ability to win quick promotion to the Deepdale club's first team where he would, in time, attract better offers from larger outfits. Willie must be mad!

Loyalty to Carlisle would be best demonstrated by giving them access to that much-needed £500. That was the financial side of the game; small clubs sold their best to bigger teams.

If it wasn't Preston, then he would be sold to the next bidder!

Willie respected his brother's points and agreed to retract his refusal but was struck by the new learning experience that footballers were no more than chattels, the property of rich men to be bought and sold as economics determined.

He was still merely a peasant whose job security, and job satisfaction, rested on the whims of the 'high and mighty' – those who controlled football clubs.

On hearing that Scott had boarded the Preston-bound express, Alec and Willie sprinted, with all the spirit of Uncle Reindeer, to Carlisle station where they only just managed to board the train.

Picking up £10 as an advance of the signing-on fee, the ticketless Shankly brothers alighted at Haltwhistle where the local stationmaster provided transfer warrants back to Carlisle. A supporter of the Brunton Park team, the poor man was not informed that young Shankly was about to move on.

Indeed, when news of Shankly's transfer reached the streets of Carlisle, locals were in uproar. Brunton Park was besieged by protesting fans who threatened to boycott future matches. It was some time before tempers calmed but many threw away their club rosettes, resolving never to return to Brunton Park.

Young Shankly had impressed the Carlisle folk through his dedication and honest application to the task. His skills on the field had brought pleasure to those requiring entertainment and excitement as a release from their daily pressures. He had become the fans' favourite. Still, as we shall see, 'their Willie' was to return to Carlisle at a later juncture in his life.

3

Proud Preston

Glenbuck villagers were quietly delighted on hearing that yet another of their young men had moved up in the soccer world. Willie, though, in true Glenbuck tradition, did not boast of his good fortune. After all, hadn't Glenbuck produced better men than himself? Didn't this village provide Scotland with internationalists and provide bigger clubs than Preston with graceful exponents of the beloved game? Shankly spent the remainder of his close-season break in Glenbuck on a self-prepared fitness programme. He encouraged the local youths to join him in training and kick-about matches. At this early age he was showing a propensity for encouraging others, organising their fitness and skills training. His brother Bob saw young Willie's future as a manager panning out before him and, jokingly, referred to the sessions as 'the Bill Shankly soccer Sunday school'.

Arriving at Deepdale in mid-July 1933, Shankly was boarded out to a local club landlady, Hannah Usher, whose task it was to help young newcomers settle in. A down-to-earth woman, Mrs Usher provided 'great digs'. Bill lodged with Hannah Usher for nine years, returning later for visits during the war years. He thought so much of Mrs Usher and her family that, later, prior to marrying, he introduced his future bride to Hannah Usher for approval, only to be told by his former landlady: 'She's too good for you, Willie Shankly.'

Shankly soon settled at Deepdale. His uncertainties and fears of the unknown soon abated. His digs were perfect with wages left over, Deepdale was a fine stadium, local people were not the big city ogres he had imagined and his self-confidence was growing.

Training sessions met with Shankly's approval. Bill Scott and his assistant trainer, Jimmy Metcalfe, knew their subject. Preston were well known as a club who placed great emphasis on skilful soccer. They had a proud tradition of turning out 'footballing stars' and were eager to continue in that vein. Discerning Preston fans demanded higher skills and artistry from their heroes.

Season 1933–34 was being heralded with great anticipation. Languishing outwith the mainstream soccer scene for almost ten years, both club and supporters were desperate to have 'Proud Preston' back in the major division, competing for Wembley glory. It was only a matter of time.

Shankly's Deepdale career began with a reserve-team debut against Blackpool's second eleven. Following several 'settling-in' reserve-team appearances, he was promoted to his first-team outing on 9 December 1933 against Hull City. A stout performance which impressed both management and fans secured Shankly regular appearances as first eleven right half-back.

Fitting in well with the Preston style of play, Shankly soon became a firm favourite of Deepdale's most loyal supporters. His first season with the Lilywhites was immensely satisfying as he had contributed well in helping the club attain their ambition of a return to First Division status as runners-up to Second Division champions Grimsby Town.

Division One wages meant a rise of £3 to £8 per week. In no time at all he had soared to victory – and there was no stopping him.

Preston were serious about making a challenge in the First Division. Their fans were hungry for a return to the days of glory and anticipated honours coming the Lancashire club's way.

Shankly's attitude to life and dedication to his sport won him admiration both on and off the field. Nothing was too much trouble for the likeable young Scot whose honesty, demeanour and good manners made an impact on those associated with Preston North End. Always first on the training pitch, eager to learn and practise new techniques, willing to lend a hand around the stadium, courteous towards the fans, he soon became an adopted son for the town which had previous connections with the lad's birthplace through former players Robert and William Blyth, Alec Brown, Robert Crawford, Peter McIntyre and Alec Tait. Glenbuck and Preston had yet again formed an association through young Willie who, conscious of this 'auld alliance', was not about to let the village, or Preston, down.

Such was the impact Shankly had on the football pitch in his first season at Deepdale that both Portsmouth and Arsenal made efforts to secure his services. Now, whilst league champions Arsenal would have been the favourites to land the promising young right-half's transfer, the offer did not come at the right time. It did not suit Preston to part company with their budding starlet who was wooing the fans to Deepdale in increasing numbers; he was an asset to the club who envisaged greater financial rewards in keeping hold of him, perhaps moving him on later for a higher reward.

Although impressed by such an interest in his abilities, Shankly was quite at home in Preston; he enjoyed footballing with the quality of players around him at Deepdale. Let the board of directors act in the interests of finance over his possible move to Arsenal, that was their way. Shankly would settle to the better way – giving 100 per cent for his club, entertaining the fans and returning the warm friendship afforded him by the good folk of Preston.

After all, whilst it would have been fine to join Arsenal, enjoying a higher status as a professional, Shankly recalled Robert Burns's words:

The rank is but the guinea's stamp,
The Man's the gowd for a' that.

Preston's first season in the First Division was pretty average. Finishing mid-table in their first season back among the top flight and reaching the FA Cup quarter-finals may have been satisfactory for some but the Deepdale faithful demanded more. Consolidating their First Division status in season 1934–35, the Lilywhites again failed in the FA Cup quarter-final stages.

Still, progress was being made, a fine young team was being assembled at Deepdale and as he had done back home in Glenbuck, Shankly was always on hand to encourage those younger than himself in developing their skills and fitness.

Preston's first team were quickly building themselves a reputation as the team to watch for the future. Shankly had built himself a reputation as a 'running machine' with uncanny positional strength. Hard in the tackle, he was a 90-minute man – stout in defence, skilled in moving forward. The short passing style at Preston suited him. Players such as Jimmy Milne and Andy Beattie joined forces with Shankly, giving Preston a quality which was to make them a force to be reckoned with in coming years.

By the end of season 1935–36, Shankly had now become recognised as one of the finest half-backs in English league football. Rarely missing through injury, his tenacity and determined approach to the game was attracting the attention of Scotland's national selectors.

Season 1936–37 saw Preston continue their development towards a recognised football force. Whilst their league form continued to be inconsistent, they were maintaining their reputation as a cup-tie team, hard to beat on the one-off big-occasion match. Disposing of Newcastle in the FA Cup third round by two goals to nil, the Lilywhites then recorded victories against Stoke City, Exeter and Tottenham Hotspur before tackling West Bromwich Albion in the semi-final at Highbury.

Preston triumphed by four goals to one and were set for

their first Wembley final appearance since 1922 against a strong Sunderland team. In this first ever May Day Wembley Cup final – moved from April as part of the celebrations to mark the coronation of King George VI – Preston's Frank O'Donnell was the first to score a goal. Although Preston completely outplayed their north-east opponents throughout the first half, the day was to end gloomily for the Deepdale fans who had made the journey south. Early second-half goals by Gurney and Raich Carter gave Sunderland the lead, which was extended by Burbanks to three goals to one in the 71st minute.

Although bitterly disappointed at this defeat in his first Wembley appearance, Shankly was first to congratulate the victors: 'We were beaten by a far superior team.'

Putting the Wembley failure behind them, Preston began a serious assault on the 1937–38 league championship with George Mutch who had joined the Deepdale ranks from Manchester United. Callimore and Beattie had settled to a full-back partnership; Shankly, Smith and Milne provided a magnificent half-back line; whilst O'Donnell, Dougal, Smith, Mutch and Maxwell provided the forward threat.

Known at this time as 'The Preston Scottish', North End boasted of no less than ten Scotsmen in their first-team pool.

Shankly was fast becoming the First Division's top wing-half. Crowds were flocking to Deepdale in record numbers to watch Willie and his 'Preston Scottish' mount their challenge. Always close to top position, the Lilywhites chased leaders Arsenal to the final game of the season when a 3–1 victory at Deepdale gave the Gunners yet another title. Preston finished third to Wolverhampton Wanderers.

The cup glory which had eluded them the previous season was, however, soon to be Preston's.

Facing Huddersfield in the 1938 Wembley final, Shankly and his Preston Scots were determined not to let the fans down yet again. Ten thousand television viewers watched the first ever FA Cup final to be broadcast live on TV. Scoreless after the first 90 minutes, the game went into extra time. With the cup-tie entering its final minute, Preston's man of the match,

Shankly, stroked a ball through to Mutch who was fouled in the penalty box by Huddersfield centre-half and captain, Alf Young.

Mutch scored from the resultant penalty and brought Cup glory back to Preston.

This was the pinnacle of Shankly's playing career, an experience he was to recapture with his Liverpool stars in years to come. Of the Preston Wembley triumph he said: 'When the whistle blows at Wembley and you've played in a final you've won, that's the greatest thrill of your life . . . No doubt about that. I thanked God for that. The feeling is unbelievable.'

There was, though, yet another unbelievable experience that season. Shankly had joined the ranks of former fellow village residents William Muir, Alec Brown, George Halley, John Crosbie and his brother Bob in being chosen to wear the dark blue for Scotland. The young lion rampant of Preston was soon to bring further distinction to Glenbuck as he embarked upon his international football career.

4

The Lion Rampant

Recognising Shankly's tremendous contribution to Preston's growing league stature and magnificent Cup runs, Scotland's selectors included the wing-half and fellow Lilywhites Mutch, Smith and Beattie in the 1938 Scotland versus England international at Wembley two weeks prior to the FA Cup final.

Some billed the match 'England versus Preston' such was the influence of Shankly's fellow Scots at Deepdale.

Although deeply proud of young Willie Shankly's inclusion against the 'Auld Enemy', Glenbuck villagers who planned to join the tartan invasion of London for the occasion were absent from his national debut!

Keen to see Shankly lift an FA Cup winners' medal later, those holding Wembley international tickets sold them and cancelled travel arrangements opting instead to cheer their lad on in his later Cup final appearance. They could only afford one Wembley trip.

Shankly was disappointed that no one from home would be there to see him in dark blue, but he understood that finances did not allow for anything else.

He described his debut as 'the greatest day of my father's life'. The rampant lion-bearing chest of this young, fiercely proud Scot, raised on the south Ayrshire moors 'amongst the greatest people on earth', swelled as he stepped onto the Wembley turf to the resounding cheers of those tartan-tammied fellows from the land o' Burns who had made the long trek to London.

Wallace and Bruce, Bannockburn, the suffering of the Scottish agricultural and mining classes at the hands of English entrepreneurs – all of these welled up in his young mind and body. He would have recalled Robert Burns:

Scots, wha hae wi' Wallace bled,
Scots, wham Bruce has aften led,
Welcome to your gory bed,–
Or to victorie.–

Bobby Reid, a fellow Scottish cap on the day, wrote: 'Bill ran till he dropped, the lion on his shirt was always tearing out for victory.'

Shankly was beside himself with joy as Heart of Midlothian's Tommy Walker scored a thundering 30-yard drive to give Scotland a 1–0 victory, sending the tartan army homewards singing their Burns ballads and Robert Wilson's popular tunes.

Shankly's display against the 'Auld Enemy' at Wembley gained him a further four caps before the outbreak of war. Northern Ireland were defeated 2–0 in Belfast in October 1938; Wales lost 3–2 at Tynecastle Park, Edinburgh, a month later; then the Magyars of Hungary were trounced by three goals to one at Ibrox, Glasgow. The rampant Scots were heading for the Home Internationals triple crown, facing England at Hampden in April 1939.

England's Lawton and Matthews, however, had other ideas. On a drenched Hampden turf, the Scots were cruising to a 1–0 victory when, in the last quarter, England's 'Terrible Two' took the game by the scruff of the neck. Beasley of Huddersfield equalised then England dashed Scotland's hopes with a stunning Lawton winner.

Once again, Shankly rose to the occasion as he

congratulated England on their victory. Nationalistic pride was one thing, but to lose to 'Lawton, a great centre-forward, and Matthews . . . we weren't beaten by nobodies, we were beaten by players'.

Shankly enjoyed his early Scotland caps. He knew how much these fixtures meant to the ordinary man, the 'Terracing Tam' who packed the lofty Hampden slopes or made the pilgrimage to away matches. The national fervour which manifested itself in these games was yet another escape for the masses' search for relief from the reality of their hard-working, grossly underpaid existences.

As with Glenbuck, Scotland was a community, albeit a larger one. Shankly had a pride in representing that community; he felt a responsibility towards the fans. If they went home happy, he and his team-mates had contributed to that happiness. If they went home sad, then he shared in that sadness. This community spirit, this eagerness to please those who counted most in football – the supporters – would in future years be demonstrated in all its glory on the terracing of Anfield, Liverpool.

This Scotland versus England encounter, though, was to prove the last full international for eight years as war loomed on the horizon.

Aged 25, Shankly feared being cut off in his prime as Hitler's war drew the curtain on organised league and cup fixtures, home internationals and friendlies with foreign nations. Although the 1939–40 season started on schedule, only a few games were played when, on 3 September, the day after Shankly's 26th birthday, the nation heard through their wireless sets, 'Britain is at war with Germany'! Initially, Shankly felt cheated. Hadn't they banned football during the First World War fearing for crowd safety and summoned all fit young men to the front?

However, recognising the impact that national sport had on morale, the Government allowed organised football to continue on a regional basis. Footballers, though, would be required to serve in the forces.

Shankly was entering a new and uncertain juncture in his

life. How could he plan for the future? What future? He didn't know it, but the dark, uncertain years ahead were to contain some of the brightest moments of his life!

5

The War Years

As Europe became engaged in the initial stages of war, Shankly and Preston became part of the Northern League, the Football League having been abandoned for the duration.

For the first time, Shankly lined up alongside Tom Finney, one of Preston's promising youths so encouraged by the Scots right-half during the previous years. Finney was emerging as one of the most brilliant footballers England had produced. Shankly had the greatest respect for the youngster whom he described later as 'the greatest footballer I ever saw'.

Finney's heading skills, his ability to dribble past defenders with ease, his ball control – all were admired by Shankly who admittedly envied the youngster's exceptional soccer talents. This admission was reciprocated by Finney, who greatly appreciated Shankly's interest in the Preston youth squad, the encouragement he had given to younger Deepdale playing staff and his positive involvement in their development.

Both players were excited at the prospect of combining forces in a squad which included the Beatties, Mutch and Dougal. Indeed, if Shankly felt that war had stunted his career, the loyal Deepdale supporters felt cheated that Preston's finest ever assembled array of talent had been denied a probable Football League and FA Cup double. They had patiently awaited the birth of an all-conquering Lilywhite side and when they arrived, Hitler's war took it away. The Preston potential was never realised!

There was, nevertheless, plenty to crow about. The Shankly/Finney inspired Preston won the Northern Regional League and also defeated Arsenal 2–1 in the 1940–41 Wartime Cup final. Not quite the real thing but then, there was a war on.

In June 1940 Shankly enlisted in the RAF. He could have returned to the pits as a 'reserved occupation worker', but opted first of all to take on a wartime job with a local builder and then as a riveter in a factory producing Hampden bombers. Oh, the irony! His enlistment in the RAF meant he could continue to play for Preston as a posting to Padgate near Warrington meant he could easily travel to Deepdale. A transfer to RAF Gosford, where it was intended that he would become a physical training instructor followed. Shankly's affinity with the common soldier, his popularity with the men, led those in charge at Gosford to the belief that he would not make NCO (non-commissioned officer) material. They drummed up the excuse that his broad Scots tongue could not be understood in the gym or parade ground! He was posted on to the balloon barrage depot in Bury, from where he continued to appear for Preston and turned out for the barrage team in the Manchester and District RAF League. It was during this time that Shankly developed a passion for boxing, winning an inter-camp trophy at light middleweight.

In November 1941, Shankly incurred the most serious injury of his football career. A suspected broken knee-cap, sustained in a Preston versus Halifax cup-tie, proved to be cartilage damage. Panic set in as an RAF medic predicted the end of Shankly's football career had arrived.

With typical dogged determination, Shankly dismissed this prognosis, continuing to train hard and play whenever he could. Settling to service life, he enjoyed his boxing and maintained a very high level of fitness.

International games to raise funds for the war effort, involving Scotland elevens against England and Army teams or 'AID' internationals, were regular occurrences. A highlight of those events for Shankly was his captaining Scotland against England at Hampden. A near-80,000 crowd were disappointed as the new skipper and his 'Bravehearts' were trounced 3–1. Revenge, however, was sweet. A year later, in a return fixture at Wembley, Shankly scored in a five goals to four victory for the Scots against an England XI containing many of their stars.

A newspaper report at the time commented: 'Shankly was a great fellow, shoulders braced, the blood of Bruce in his veins, and the skill of the football ace in his feet.'

With clothing in short supply during the war years, Scotland's kit was provided by Heart of Midlothian's Tommy Walker, who kitted out his team-mates with a selection of strips collected during his international career. Shankly greatly admired Walker's unselfishness.

Shankly's knee injury was playing up despite his stoical efforts to 'play down the fuss'. Inevitably, Scotland insisted that he prove his fitness before being selected for a 1944 international against England at Wembley. He was asked to test his suspect knee by kicking a goalpost during a training session at Stamford Bridge on the eve of the international.

Shankly refused point blank, saying 'he wouldn't do nothing so stupid even with the good leg'.

Wartime matches at Preston had come to an end in the '40s as Deepdale had been commandeered for military purposes. Postings to several camps in England and Wales, however, led to the right-half turning out for Luton, Liverpool, Cardiff, Norwich, Bolton and Arsenal.

He played a major part in Arsenal reaching the 1943 League Cup final South, to be staged at Wembley, and was eagerly anticipating a return to the stadium when Arsenal, a club whose professionalism, high standards and facilities greatly impressed Shankly, delivered one of the greatest upsets of his life.

Having helped the Gunners secure that season's Football League South title, Shankly, quite rightly, expected to be included in the Wembley final line-up. Keen to secure the

Cup, though, Arsenal used all their influence to draw in their great players who were, as serving soldiers, stationed throughout the UK. As a 'guest', Shankly was dropped. To add insult to injury, Highbury directors offered their guesting right-half tickets to the all-London final against Charlton and 'expenses' to compensate for his disappointment.

The proud Scot was livid! Favouritism, disloyalty and picking players for sentimental reasons stuck in his craw. In later years, as a manager, he would never allow these feelings to cloud his own judgement – he had experienced the pain of rejection a footballer suffered when he had given his all, only to be replaced, by all accounts, by a lesser talent. Typically, Shankly watched the Cup final from the terraces with a ticket he had purchased himself. Arsenal won the Cup. The Scot was denied a medal, for which he never forgave the Londoners. He had, however, learned yet another lesson in life which would stand him in good stead later!

It was during the war years that Shankly developed his famous 'Jimmy Cagney swagger'. He was thrilled by the actor's gangster roles on the cinema screen. Wasn't Cagney around the same height? Wasn't there a facial similarity? Wasn't he a tough guy like Willie? Cagney became Shankly's screen idol, his hero. As a star with Preston, and then with a host of wartime sides including the mighty Arsenal, wasn't he entitled (albeit completely out of character for a native of Glenbuck) to swagger a little?

During those years, wherever he was posted, the football 'star' also involved himself with local youths – coaching, organising matches, encouraging young lads in the great game. All who came into contact with the man during his national service remember him as 'a stout fellow, honest and diligent', keen to help his fellow man in any situation. 'When you made Shankly's acquaintance, you had met a friend in the true sense of the word,' testified old buddy Frank Curry.

Home beckoned in September 1943 when a posting to Scotland led Shankly to Bishopbriggs in Glasgow. His father John was dying and the short train journey from Glasgow to Ayrshire would allow the youngest son to pay his respects and see to family matters.

Word of Shankly's coming soon reached the directors of Partick Thistle FC who, keen to beat Rangers and Celtic in signing the accomplished wing-half, wasted no time in rushing to meet him as he arrived at Central Station.

The 'Jags' were operating a strong youth policy in preparation for a return to post-war football and saw Shankly as the ideal mentor for their raw, developing lads.

Thistle were good to Shankly. They funded a £150 cartilage removal at a private Glasgow nursing home and treated him with the utmost respect. A debut against Dumbarton in October 1943 proved disastrous, Thistle being trounced by six goals to two. Shankly pulled up his sleeves: there was a lot to be done. Coaxing, cajoling and encouraging, he guided his young Firhill team-mates through a string of victories. On one notable fixture, Shankly thundered a four-yard drive past Rangers goalkeeper and fellow cap Jerry Dawson, earning Thistle a 3–3 draw at Ibrox.

Shankly and his 'Jags' went on that season to defeat classy Hibernian, with their host of wartime 'guests', in the summer Cup final, recording a shock 2–0 victory.

Shankly never forgot Thistle's kindness towards him. Whilst the high and mighty had asked him to test his injured knee by kicking a goalpost, the Firhill directors had raised the necessary funds to have the injury explored properly and, to a great extent, rectified.

The 'Maryhill Magyars' would always have a special place in his heart.

6

Bonnie Ness

During his convalescence from the cartilage operation, Shankly and a friend, services heavyweight champion boxer Jock Porter, would jog around camp at Bishopbriggs.

As he and Jock took off, in all weathers, to run the roads and lanes surrounding the camp, a young WRAF signals operator would glance though her window near the camp guardroom, wondering who these athletes were and what they were up to.

These two 'joggers' seemed free to come and go as they pleased, merely nodding to officers as they went on their way. On being told that the smaller, 'and better looking' one, was the footballer Bill Shankly, Ness merely shrugged her shoulders. 'I knew nothing of football nor who Shankly was. I thought he was a nutcase running out in rain and sleet.'

On hearing that an attractive young WRAF had been enquiring about him, Shankly wasted no time in introducing himself. Her name was Agnes Fisher and he immediately fell in love with her. She, however, couldn't stand the coarse, seemingly arrogant, athlete who swaggered around like James Cagney. With typical Ayrshire stubbornness, Shankly relentlessly pursued young 'Ness' Fisher, but not with the flowers or chocolates we might expect. His 'romanticism' was more down to earth: laden with slices of toasted cheese, Shankly persistently beat a well-trodden path to Ness's billet until 'he gradually wore me down'.

The couple found they had something in common. Ness, too, had been awarded a compassionate posting to Bishopbriggs to be near her dying mother in Glasgow. They comforted each other in their respective grief.

Spending leaves together, Shankly and Ness soon fell deeply in love. Desperate to have Ness witness his footballing skills, Shankly pleaded with her to attend matches. At first she refused, having no interest in sport, but relented when her sick father said: 'He's a nice boy. Just please him and go to a match.'

Wincing at the crunching tackles in Thistle's matches at Ibrox and Parkhead, Ness felt 'these mad footballers were merely out to do damage to each other – or worse'.

Having met Ness's parents, Shankly proudly took her down to Glenbuck 'to meet the family'. Although she found the Glenbuck 'clan' somewhat different from her fellow Glaswegians, Ness took to the Shanklys; they, in turn, welcomed Willie's fiancée with open arms – and hearts.

The couple were married in Glasgow on 29 June 1944 – outwith the football season at Bill's insistence! Following the church wedding in Glasgow, a reception was held in Glenbuck where the remaining villagers were deeply proud of their footballing genius and his attractive new bride.

Thankful to Shankly for his sterling efforts at Firhill during the war years, the Partick Thistle Supporters Club arranged a leaving reception for Mr and Mrs Shankly. Over 1,000 fans crowded into Grove boxing stadium where the newlyweds were presented with a canteen of cutlery and silver cake stand. These gifts meant the world to Shankly – more than medals – since they had come from honest, working-class folk who had scraped together their pennies and ha'pennies to make donations in appreciation of his endeavours on their behalf. To be rewarded by ordinary folk in the street was the greatest accolade of all. This sentiment would be passed on to future generations of footballers under Shankly's management.

As peace returned, the Shanklys welcomed their first-born. Before leaving Glasgow to return to Deepdale, the proud Shankly held his daughter Barbara in his arms. Born in Glasgow in the summer of 1945, baby Barbara was her father's pride and joy. Ness recalled: 'He loved Barbara, he was delighted to be a father and was devoted to her.'

Yes, the war years had been filled with many new experiences for Shankly. He had learned a lot and would carry that learning – those experiences – into this new stage in his life.

Some dark days still lay ahead but the footballing Scot now had the reinforcement of a loving, caring wife and new-born child to carry him through. He also had greater responsibilities.

7

Proud Preston – Poor People

Following the euphoric post-war celebrations, British soccer began to boom. Stadiums were packed to capacity as league football proper recommenced on Saturday, 31 August 1946. Whilst the turnstiles clicked, clocking up record attendances at most grounds, the clubs were undergoing periods of reorganisation, laying blueprints for the seasons to come. Many former players had passed their peaks during the war years, some had been killed or injured in action, hundreds had drifted out of the game, their careers abruptly ended due to the conflict.

When Shankly returned to Deepdale following demobilisation, Preston directors had strong reservations about his ability to pick up where he had left off. In his mid-thirties now, with a wife and child, and nursing a weak knee, was he any longer an asset to the club? This attitude from a club for which he gave so much, hurt Shankly who, in typically dogged fashion, set out to prove his detractors wrong.

The Shankly family secured a small terraced house in Deepdale Road and the breadwinner set out to work.

'He's past his best,' they said. 'He's older now.'

Shankly ignored these remarks and set about the task at hand with all the old celtic fire he could summon.

Again, teaming up with Finney, Beattie and old comrades, Shankly helped Preston maintain their First Division status. Preston directors, however, were dissatisfied with their seventh-place position and sixth-round FA Cup exit at the hands of Lancashire rivals, Manchester United.

On his 35th birthday, Shankly was told that first-team football at Preston was no longer an option: he should consider himself a second-team man. A younger team was being assembled. His popularity with the fans and staff, however, was seen as an important asset by Preston directors keen to keep morale up as they struggled towards higher ground.

Young Tommy Finney was benefiting greatly from the older 'warhorse's' presence at Deepdale. With an air of resignation, Shankly accepted his lot. His playing days were nearly over. Due to the war he had, as had so many others, been cheated of a glittering career where medals, caps and accolades in greater number than he had amassed could have been his. After 16 years of loyalty, he expected Preston to have stood firmly behind him, yet here they were saying 'it's good to have you around – but not in a jersey'. With his family responsibilities, Shankly looked to the future. If first-team football was out, he would find another source of employment in his beloved sport.

Preston offered Shankly a three-year contract coaching the reserves and youth teams, but the proud Scot felt he had more to offer the game. Why should he listen to bloated, self-opinionated directors whose main interest was the club's bank account. When had they ever pounded the turf; sweated for the jersey? Just who did they think they were dealing with?

The shoulders were shrugged Cagney style. Shankly knew within himself that the stuff which pulsated through his veins was the bloodstock of a hardy race. As an Ayrshireman, he knew he had more commitment, loyalty and compassion in his little finger than these 'pillars of Preston society' had in their whole bodies.

He was still a young man and would go on in the game to show these people – lawyers, butchers, bakers, grocers and other such investors – that this sport was more than a capital venture. Not for him demotion into obscurity when the people's game needed sorting out!

He enjoyed a spell coaching the Preston youths and took a correspondence course in physiotherapy. Preston offered him a position as club reserve team coach, scout and physio. Disenchanted with this offer, however, Shankly used his remaining time at Deepdale to gain the experience necessary for moving on, but not before he had settled a financial score.

After 16 years, Shankly felt he was due a large retirement benefit. Playing in that post-war era entitled a player to a benefit of £150 per annum if he had served five consecutive years with the same club. £750 was not an unreasonable sum in those days. Nevertheless, having played over 300 league and cup games at Deepdale, Shankly felt he was entitled to a bit more. After all, he had laboured on only the average footballer's pay and had dropped considerably to service pay for six years.

An offer was made whereby a testimonial match plus full benefit pay-out would come Shankly's way were he to agree to stay at Deepdale in the new reserve coach/physio role. The catch was that he had to remain at Deepdale in this new position under a three-year contract. Shankly was incensed. Preston had no need of him as a first-team player but were ensuring no one else could have his services. They knew that several clubs were interested in securing the Scot's services as player-manager. Mighty Preston wasn't so mighty when it came to loyalty and just rewards to long-serving Deepdale staff!

Feeling swindled, Shankly agreed to an offer by Carlisle United, announced his retirement as a player and took up the position of manager at Brunton Park on 19 March 1949.

On hearing of Shankly's leaving, and the bitter circumstances surrounding his move, the Deepdale faithful rallied, raising a collection of £169 5s 7d. A gesture by the fans both in appreciation of Shankly's service to Preston and as a snub to the club's directors whom the ordinary supporters felt had let down their reputation as proud Preston by their meanness towards a club hero.

Shankly said of this gesture: 'Supporters go on forever, but directors can be gone in a month.' On his retirement many tributes were paid to Shankly by players, former opponents, managers and fans of numerous league clubs. The common folk of Preston rallied to wish the new manager well in the task that lay ahead at Carlisle.

Long-time opponent Joe Mercer wrote to him: 'I must write you a few lines of congratulations and good wishes on your recent appointment. I hope most sincerely that your career as a manager will be even more successful than that as player. In my humble opinion, no player ever gave as much to his club, country and football as you.'

Many such testimonials were received. Ness began packing for a move which would not be the last in the Shankly family's lives.

As he looked back, Shankly allowed himself a wry smile when in May 1949 Preston were relegated.

It was the poor people who ran Preston North End, the proud who supported. The same amateur board of directors who knew nothing of football and had shown a complete lack of integrity in dealing with Shankly had plunged the Lilywhites back into Second Division football. So be it!

8

Back to Carlisle

On 22 March 1949, Shankly was officially appointed manager of Carlisle United FC, replacing Ivor Broadis, who had moved from Brunton Park to Sunderland as player–manager for a fee of £18,000.

Carlisle were keen to have the services of a young 'tracksuit' manager, fresh into retirement from playing, and felt their former wing-half could bring the crowds flocking in once again. A salary equivalent to what was on offer at Preston was enough to entice the Scot northwards. Carlisle was also within easy travelling distance of Glenbuck and Glasgow. With his uncle Bill Blyth still around, Shankly felt he and the family would have a settled time as he embarked upon his first managerial role, serving his 'gaffer's' apprenticeship at the helm of a club.

Ness and Barbara returned to Glasgow for a short while until a family house was secured in Carlisle.

Taking over with just seven league games remaining in the Third Division North, Shankly brought his first trophy to Brunton Park, winning the Cumbrian Cup in his first year of tenure. The first season petered out quietly, Carlisle consolidating their position in the league though finishing in the bottom half.

With Britain still in the grip of austerity, the 'escape' of football was still highly popular. Attendances at league and cup fixtures continued to boom. The 'away supporter' had not yet been invented: the fact that petrol continued to be rationed, access to cars was limited and insufficient wages made long-distance coach or rail travel quite impossible, resulted in townsfolk congregating at their local stadium for any away fixtures. The local club became an integral part of community life.

Carlisle United would become a community based on the Glenbuck model, where neighbours relied upon each other, where a victory for one was a victory for all. A community where the virtues of honest endeavour and loyalty were paramount. The club would represent the whole people and would bring them the escape they sought – thrills, entertainment and enjoyment. Players would be proud to play for the club, proud in the knowledge that they were providing a vital service to the community.

An initial step towards installing this pride was the purchase of new kit – if you were representing the folk of Carlisle, you would be 'well turned out'. Old John's earlier lesson was manifesting itself!

Brunton Park stadium was in the same state of dilapidation as it was when Shankly left all those years ago. If the club was to become a focal point for Carlisle citizens, then a tidying-up operation was needed. From the terracings to the dressing-rooms, players and volunteer supporters, led by the new 'gaffer', embarked upon a spring cleaning and refurbishment of the stadium.

Shankly led this industrious workforce as it set to with brooms, paint brushes, hammers, nails and saws. The door of the new manager's office was always open. Supporters were encouraged to come along and discuss club affairs. It was also at this juncture that Shankly's relationship with the media began to develop.

'Transparent management' had arrived. Shankly firmly believed that accessibility to the inner sanctums of the club by the common people and the press would engender a feeling of togetherness, all having a responsibility for the well-being of the operation at Brunton Park.

The first new signing during the early days was Shankly's former Preston team-mate Paddy Waters. On first signing at Brunton Park, Waters thought Shankly was mad. This little outfit was surely going nowhere. Summoning up all his powers of persuasion, however, Shankly, enticed the talented, if ageing, Dublin-born wing-half into joining United. Other signings included Billy Hogan from Manchester City and Geoff Twentyman – later to rejoin Shankly in Liverpool. George Dick was signed from West Ham as Carlisle's first team was assembled around tried and trusted veterans and emerging juniors from Scotland.

Carlisle's directors were persuaded to invest in town flats to provide cheap rented accommodation as an incentive to those wishing to join the Brunton Park playing staff.

Unqualified as a coach, Shankly preached a simple gospel to his squad. 'Football is a simple game . . . Get the basics right and you're away.'

Road running, a feature of training in those days, was banned. Rather than an endurance test, fitness training was to be an enjoyable experience with a variety of stamina-building exercises designed to make it more interesting.

Using his influence around town, Shankly arranged with employers that part-time members of the squad would have time off to participate in daily sessions with full-timers.

A new concept was introduced – ball-work. Shankly wasn't interested in seeing his squad sprint up and down terraces or jog incessantly around the cinder track pitch perimeter. Soccer was played with a ball. Didn't the all-conquering post-war Hungarians concentrate on ball skills?

'You play on grass, you'll train on grass,' his players were told. 'You'll work hard on your fitness but then you'll be expected to spend hours on ball skills, head-work, throw-ins, corners and all aspects of your game.'

Natural ability was encouraged whilst players were urged to cultivate their talents with all the energy and pride they could summon. The Shankly system of coaching also involved

hour upon hour of five-a-side games, head-tennis competitions and continuous ball playing.

'I don't want them running up and down the terracing, the
fans can do that. Here we play with a ball, we'll train with a
ball.' Revolutionary indeed, in post-war British football
coaching.

A tremendous team spirit developed at Carlisle where
competition for first-team inclusion was fierce. A strong
reserve team was assembled, Shankly believing that his first-
team regulars would be more determined in their efforts if a
promising young protégé was snapping at their heels.

Another communications innovation developed by Shankly
at Brunton Park was his own 'Clubcall'. Ahead of his time,
the manager took to commandeering the club's loudspeaker
system to talk to supporters before kick-off. Using the
medium of the microphone, he would announce the day's
teams, inform supporters of club business and generally chat
about aspects of football. These 'Shankly Calling' sessions
were a favourite with the crowds, many of whom came along
specifically to hear the broadcasts.

Shankly's direct appeal to the fans was phenomenal: 'I'm
not appealing for support, we get ample support already. I
just want to take the crowd into the club's confidence and let
them know what's happening.'

Within a couple of months Shankly had Carlisle abuzz with
anticipation about the fortunes of United. A 'feel-good' factor
had been created around the club. Using new-found media
and communications skills, he became his and the club's own
spin-doctor, convincing all around that, with a concerted
effort, Carlisle United could rise to the highest pinnacle in
their 18 years' existence.

His hand was firmly at the helm. Not a day passed without
the new manager involving himself in even the smallest aspect
of the club's affairs. Within the town he was creating an
atmosphere of confidence. Locals believed that they had a
messiah whose confidence and commitment would put United
on the soccer map.

The 'big wooden rabbit hutch' which was Brunton Park,

was gleaming. By all accounts, training and coaching sessions were more modern; the team was well turned out. Surely the results would come as Shankly brought in his first signing.

Carlisle, though, was a soccer outpost. The north-west railway town didn't readily attract eager youngsters embarking upon their footballing careers. Nor older hands stepping down a division. Things were on the way up, but the fans were cautioned that the 'revolution may take a couple of seasons'!

By now, a football-mad Carlisle was flocking to Brunton Park. Crowds of 15 to 18 thousand were commonplace as the Blues entered season 1949–50. 'Organised football, played properly to the maximum effort', would bring results, according to Shankly who would announce through the loudspeaker system: 'The boys are going to give their best. There are one or two locals in today's team, so cheer them on.'

Carlisle were somewhat isolated geographically, facing long journeys to away fixtures in pre-motorway England. Always positive, Shankly turned this situation into an asset by telling players that opposition teams, unused to such long treks, would be exhausted by the time they reached Brunton Park. 'Fortress Brunton', with its football-mad home support, would provide a daunting experience for opponents.

Season '49–'50 started well but travelling to away fixtures began to take its toll. Although performing well at home, Carlisle players began to show signs of travel weariness, winning only a handful of away fixtures.

The Carlisle town badge and motto, 'Be Just and Fear Not', was incorporated onto the club's jerseys as a further demonstration that Carlisle United were the town's representatives when on duty. Publicans and hoteliers were told to keep an eye out for errant players who might stray towards a pint or two.

Such was Shankly's commitment that Ness recalled him purchasing a large Bendix washing machine on the club's account and installing it at home to ensure the strips were laundered to perfection. In a season of reorganisation,

Carlisle finished ninth, a little better than the previous year.

Season tickets for the 1950–51 campaign rose to record levels. Everyone in Carlisle wanted to be associated with the great infectious wave of optimism being created by Shankly. Although the club again failed to win promotion, an exciting season saw them attain a final position of third, their highest ever league placing.

There was high drama in the FA Cup that season when, following wins over Barrow and Southport, Shankly's troops were drawn against mighty Arsenal at Highbury. With typical use of psychology, Shankly, predicting victory for Carlisle, announced to the media: 'Arsenal? Who are Arsenal? Never heard of them!'

English football was stunned as Shankly's boys held the mighty Gunners to a 0–0 draw in London. Hopes were high in Carlisle that United could finish off their mighty opponents at 'Fortress Brunton Park'. As his players stripped for the occasion, Shankly burst into the dressing-room announcing excitedly: 'Boys, I've just seen them getting out of their coach. They should be in hospital; they're in a right state. The centre forward can hardly walk.'

This rubbishing of opponents to build up his own players' confidence was to become a feature of the Shankly system at Liverpool a decade later.

Nevertheless, Arsenal's quality began to show through as the game wore on. Whilst United gave a fine account of themselves, the Gunners ran out 4–1 winners, having provided a capacity crowd at Brunton Park with a great afternoon's entertainment.

'Boys,' said Shankly after the tie, 'you've just lost to the greatest side in England – but it took them two games.' Even in defeat, the Carlisle boys' chests swelled with pride.

The railway town stage was far too small for Shankly and he was never going to be Carlisle's for long.

After two exciting seasons, during which they almost gained promotion to the Second Division, it was obvious that financial constraints surrounding the club meant that

Shankly's aspirations of creating a top-class side competing at a higher level couldn't become reality.

Grimsby Town had been watching Shankly's initial attempt at management, and liked his style and its results. The Mariners were keen to have his services.

During 1951, Liverpool invited the Carlisle manager to be interviewed for their vacant managerial position. Shankly was convinced he had secured the job but fate had it otherwise. On hearing of the post being offered to Don Welsh, Shankly asked: 'Is he a mason?' Told yes, he retorted: 'That's how he got the job.'

Tears were shed by thousands as Shankly, yet again, prepared to uproot his family and move on. Ness now had two children, with Jeanette arriving on the scene in Carlisle. 'We wondered what was in store for the family as we packed for the journey to north Lincolnshire.' With typical loyalty to her man, though, and confidence in his abilities, Ness braced herself for life in new surroundings once more.

Shankly's leaving Carlisle was quite amicable. The people knew he was destined for better things. Today at Brunton Park, the memory of Willie Shankly's Carlisle contribution lives on. The town of Carlisle is deeply proud of its association with the Scot as both player and manager. He brought them dignity, and in the depression of post-war England, gave them hope.

One favourite Carlisle story is of the time Shankly encountered a group of young schoolboys in a town centre chip shop. Having seen to it that he and the lads were well stocked with piping-hot bags of chips, they sat for hours on the pavement outside the chippie, the youngsters' eyes popping, their hearts filling with pride as United's manager told of how he and his players would bring soccer glory to the town, rising to the greatest heights. The boys trotted home to dream of days when Brunton Park would become a super stadium brimming over with crowds of 50,000, cheering on the Blues as they destroyed the visiting Tottenham, Arsenal and Manchester teams.

At least, for a short while, he gave these boys a dream. One day, children in far-off Liverpool would be offered the same dream – only to have it realised!

9

Gone Fishing

Grimsby Town were delighted at having snapped up the services of Shankly. Blundell Park had once hosted First Division league football and, although having just been relegated to the Third Division North, Grimsby Town FC aspired to return quickly to greater heights.

Supporters, however, were quite cynical. Had they not seen Grimsby, over the seasons, slip into the doldrums? How would a rookie manager from the outpost of Carlisle change the club's fortunes?

A dock town, where industry mainly consisted of fishing and the nearby post-war boom of Cleethorpes as a holiday resort, Grimsby had all but given up on its local club. Morale at Blundell Park was at an all-time low, with players and staff merely going through the motions of belonging to a football club.

In typical fashion, Shankly breathed new life into the place. Within a week of arriving, his infectious enthusiasm took hold. But not everybody was enthusiastic. The chief groundsman became upset when Shankly insisted that all training take place on the grass pitch. Directors were nonplussed to discover that they were banned from the players' dressing-room. Again, with limited funds, Shankly immediately set about bringing in new faces to bolster a depleted side whose best players had recently been sold to other clubs. Jimmy Hernon was signed from Bolton, Walter Galbraith from New Brighton and Bill Brown from Queen of the South: men with reputations, tried and tested yeomen brought in to give support to developing youth.

Time was short. Shankly knew that if he were to gain promotion to the higher leagues, this would have to be achieved within a couple of seasons or Grimsby would fade into obscurity.

His first-team pool was ageing; he would have to rekindle their fires and keep them going while younger signings were sought and recruited. Repeating the style adopted at Carlisle, Shankly soon had Grimsby playing as a unit. Once again, the microphone was commandeered. The media courted the 'spin doctoring' used to motivate a club and town.

Coaxing, cajoling and encouraging his players, Shankly continued his psychology of rubbishing opponents. 'So-and so's limping.' 'Their centre-half won't last 90 minutes.' 'The goalie's hand's bandaged' – and, to a raw, juvenile goalkeeper, 'Don't worry, son, be brave. If a forward breaks through, just run to the edge of the box, arms flailing, and shout, "Shoot, you bastard. Shoot!" just like Sam Bartram used to.' The young keeper, inspired by this 'coaching', kept a clean sheet for seven weeks.

Shankly's training sessions with the emphasis on ball-work and carefully rehearsed moves attracted the attention of Matt Busby, who sent a camera crew from Manchester United to film a Grimsby workout. The Blundell Park manager, on hearing of the camera crew's presence, quickly despatched them back to Old Trafford saying: 'Work out your own tactics.'

Losing only nine league matches in his first season, Shankly took his Grimsby side to within three points of promotion, finishing second to neighbours Lincoln City, who also halted the Mariners' Cup aspirations, defeating them 3–1 in the FA Cup second round.

Shankly's charisma soon had the crowds flocking back to Blundell Park. During season 1952–53, attendance had more than doubled, with crowds of 15,000 to 20,000 packing the stadium. Shankly's philosophy was simple: pack them in at the turnstiles, and buy new players with the revenue raised.

He was desperate to bolster his ageing side with some younger blood whilst the youngsters being attracted to Grimsby were gradually brought in in preparation for greater things.

At the close of season '52–'53, Grimsby were at a crossroads. Despite generating an interest in the club using the skills he had developed at Carlisle, Shankly needed money to be made available for new players to continue the momentum.

Grimsby's board, though, were not keen to provide such finance to the manager who had brightened the stadium, raised the club's and the town's self-esteem and become immensely popular with the local citizenry. Things were fine, they said; money was being made; perhaps he was rushing things. Shankly's second season at Grimsby ended with the club dropping to seventh in the league and once again a third-round FA Cup exit at the hands of Bury.

Whilst Shankly was only too keen to work extremely long hours, involving himself in all aspects of running the club and dedicating himself to the cause of bringing glory to Blundell Park, he expected some commitment from the owners at least. It became apparent to him that Grimsby's cynicism, their lack of ambition and the board's total reluctance to plough necessary finance into building a team worthy of competing at a level which the supporters deserved, was an insurmountable obstacle.

Once again, amateurs in control were dashing the fans' hopes and stunting the growth of a club with great potential, through their reluctance to part with cash given at the turnstiles by people who shared a dream.

Shankly's spirits were at a low ebb. At home, Ness, too, was rather unsettled. Trips back home to Glasgow or Glenbuck with the children had proved difficult from Lincolnshire. She missed her family contacts and was concerned about the loss of her husband's usual sparkle and jauntiness.

Shankly was a truthful man. Didn't he hail from Glenbuck? What would be the point in harnessing all his energies to take the people of Grimsby along a road he was not sure of himself? He couldn't lie to the people, the working class.

If Grimsby Town were to continue with a lower division team due to the lack of finance to bring in new players, then it had to be made known. If the club's directors had no ambition to better the club and, consequently, the town, what was the point of him being manager of such an outfit?

Shankly's sparkle had indeed begun to wane; this lack of enterprise at Grimsby was depressing to a manager whose maxim was about keeping others' heads up and instilling confidence and self-belief in his staff.

Following the coronation of 1953, Shankly tried to summon up all his strength to tackle the '53–'54 season with a squad which he knew would give of their best but bring little reward to a faithful following. Loyal to his players and the fans, Shankly attempted to carry on despite the adversity. In turn, the team's poor performances that season were blamed by the board on the manager's failings – namely his failure to adopt proper tactics. It was hinted that the players had no respect for their 'gaffer'. Players' indiscipline due to the absence of a firm hand was said to be an instrumental factor in dropped points. An impasse had been reached. Without the support and confidence of the Grimsby board, Shankly knew that his days at Blundell Park were drawing to a close.

He had received offers from several other clubs and had nearly gone to Middlesbrough where, no doubt, a meeting with Boro's rising young starlet Brian Clough would have been interesting.

Over Christmas and New Year of 1953–54, Shankly pondered the future.

Grimsby were keen to retain him but on the condition that he 'pull himself together' and build a team within the scant resources the board felt they could allow. It was too late, however. He had decided to move on.

Feeling betrayed yet again by a board of directors, Shankly

made it known that a cash bonus, promised to him were Grimsby Town to reach the top three in their division during his first year at the helm, had not been paid. The real bone of contention, however, was the back-stabbing by directors keen to save face with supporters by blaming their manager for poor team performances, when they well knew that their lack of financial commitment was shackling the manager. This led to Shankly's resignation in the New Year of 1954.

Shankly wasn't interested in merely playing along, taking the wages whilst fawning to directors. The ordinary people who paid their hard-earned shillings to escape from their lot by passing through the turnstiles were his main consideration.

How could he con these people by giving them false hope and still hold up his head in Grimsby?

What would they have thought in Glenbuck of a man who did not give his all; who did not act honourably at all times and who simply went along with things to secure his own pay-day?

No, sir! It was time to move on.

10

Shankly by Gaslight

On 6 January Shankly moved into the manager's office at Workington Town AFC, only the second man to occupy the 'gaffer's' chair at Borough Park in Town's short two-year existence in the Football League.

Having finished bottom of the Third Division North in their inaugural season in the league, Town were flagging at second from the bottom when their new manager appeared on the scene.

Two things the Workington directors had omitted to mention to Shankly were the facts that Town shared their ground with the local rugby league club and that the stadium was heated and lit by gas! Shankly's first day at Borough Park was one of revelation: 'I opened the door, put my hand to the wall and was feeling around. A fellow said to me, "What are you doing?" "I'm putting on the light," I said. "There's gas in here," said the fellow. "Bloody gas!" I said.'

On hearing noises outside, Shankly asked a group of players what they were doing.

'We're scrumming,' was the reply.

What had he come to?

Although conditions at Workington were spartan, Shankly felt something could be accomplished. In an honest attempt to improve things on the pitch, Town had brought in some new signings. There was a loyal, hard-working supporters' club ever keen to lend a hand. A club house was secured for the family. Ness and the children found travelling from the north-west to family in Scotland easier.

Sleeves rolled up, Shankly began again to invest his energies in all aspects of the club.

Workington had a population of 30,000; the challenge ahead was to woo some of them from the town's first love of rugby league. Fund-raising activities were organised by the loyal band of supporters who also eagerly turned out in force when a lick of paint, terracing rebuilding, glazing or brickwork was required.

Shankly's arrival at Borough Park had a tremendous effect on his playing staff who, responding positively to the enthusiasm of their manager, clawed their way out of relegation trouble, and finished a mighty 20th out of 25 in the league by the end of the 1953–54 season.

Shankly spent his close-season summer restructuring and adding to Town's playing staff. New training methods were introduced as the new 'gaffer' started to get things going, using all his communication skills and powers of persuasion.

As it had been at other clubs, Shankly's enthusiasm and optimism began to rub off on others. Crowds began flocking to Borough Park – mainly to see what all the fuss was about. Shankly's boys did not let them down as, during season 1954–55, the soccer minnows rose to the giddy heights of eighth position in their division.

One famous Shankly incident occurred at this time. Travelling to London where they were due to meet mighty Leyton Orient in an FA Cup second-round tie, Workington shared their train journey with the famous Hungarian side of the '50s, who were returning to London having beaten Scotland 4–2 in an international at Hampden Park.

On hearing of the mighty Magyars' presence aboard the London-bound express, Shankly took his squad along the corridors to meet the celebrated Puskas and his comrades. Having introduced the players to each other, Shankly obtained the autographs of Puskas, Hideguti, Kosics and others before informing the Hungarians of Town's impending Cup battle in London.

Spending the remainder of the journey in each other's company, Shankly's squad and the Magyars got on like a house on fire.

Workington's 1–0 defeat of Orient, the Cup upset of the season, was typically attributed by Shankly to his introducing his players to their new-found Eastern European friends who, on hearing of Town's famous victory, sent a telegram to Borough Park which read: 'Congratulations Workington on their historic win over Leyton Orient.'

That journey, on the Flying Scotsman, had, according to Shankly, inspired his men to such a degree that 'they would have been invincible that day'.

Town's Cup run, however, was short-lived: Luton Town thrashed them by five goals to nil in the following round. But a high league placing and the FA Cup run were having their desired effect nevertheless.

The Town reserve team, known as 'the Shankly Babes', were displaying such skill and artistry that they were attracting home crowds of 3,000-plus. The rugby men were astonished at such support for local football!

Youngsters flocked to Borough Park in their droves, eager to join the Shankly school. Local amateur clubs and schools teams were drawn under the Workington Town umbrella as Shankly strove to find the best of north-west talent.

West Cumberland responded enthusiastically to Town's rising fortunes. The mainly agricultural and light engineering class, however, had no delusions of grandeur: they were being well entertained in return for their entrance fee and respected this. And who knows if promotion would come Town's way? It would be tremendous if it did, given the club's faltering start.

Shankly knew himself that money wasn't going to be made available at Workington to build a squad capable of competing in higher leagues. He was happy in his work, though, and had created change.

Prior to his arrival, the directors selected the first team. That practice stopped immediately. The board were also persuaded to pay players the £14 weekly full-time minimum wage and bonuses.

Never under contract at Borough Park, Shankly knew he would be using the time there to recharge his batteries and rekindle his own energies before moving on. His decision to leave was expedited following yet another boardroom dust-up concerning finance.

At the start of season 1955–56, Town were sitting in the league's top four and challenging well. Promotion was a realistic prospect and new players were needed if that dream was to materialise.

Once again, Shankly was subjected to the penny-pinching attitude of a hand-wringing board who informed him that, despite the club's success on the field, its growing assets and huge attendance at home games, club finances were 'not all that healthy'! If money was to be made available to him then, perhaps, this should be raised through charging more at the turnstiles or, indeed, cutting players' wages and bonuses.

That was the last straw. Once again Shankly had gone as far as he could. Did those directors really want promotion for the club, or was its success to be measured merely by financial rewards accrued in their own backyard?

With Workington flying high in the league, Shankly took a couple of days off, at the invitation of his former team-mate Andy Beattie, to participate in a testimonial match at Huddersfield Town where Beattie was manager.

Overjoyed at the prospect of playing again in front of a huge crowd, Shankly set off for Huddersfield where Beattie, in need of a quality coach and assistant manager, convinced his fellow Scot to join forces with him at the First Division club.

Had Workington's directors agreed to fund a £10,000 stadium and coaching ground improvement plan, and released some cash for players in Town's promotion run-in, Shankly would have stuck to his task at Borough Park, but it was not to be.

Although they were devastated at his decision to leave, Town parted company amicably with Shankly. So much respect did the West Cumbrians have for the man, that they were to invite him back, in later years, to Borough Park to officiate at the opening of the stadium's Bill Shankly Lounge.

11

'Forget Your Strengths, Work on Your Weaknesses'

Andy Beattie had been impressed with Shankly's ability to communicate with and encourage younger players during the Preston days. Huddersfield Town had enjoyed great success during the '20s and '30s but had struggled more recently, having been relegated to Division Two in season 1951–52, regaining promotion the following year, however, to their accustomed Division One status. The Leeds Road club were again struggling during season 1955–56 and Beattie needed help if Huddersfield were to escape the drop for the second time in four years.

Shankly's task was to bring on the club's reserve team, providing Beattie with a pool to fall back on in the event of first-team injuries. He would be responsible for recruiting youths and developing future stars. This he did, but Beattie, unfortunately, was unable to arrest his first-team's league decline.

He and his new assistant had several disagreements as Shankly often criticised first-team tactics, training methods or team selection. His criticisms were met with constant reminders by his manager, however, that his area of operation was with the reserves and that he should concentrate all his energies on that particular area.

As the first team faltered towards relegation, Shankly's 'babes' came on in leaps and bounds, a situation which was not to go unnoticed by Huddersfield's directors and supporters.

Young guns such as Denis Law, Mike O'Grady and Ray Wilson, who were to become future internationalists and football idols, were members of Shankly's Huddersfield 'babes' who were taking reserve football by storm.

As Beattie struggled, Shankly immersed himself in the task of supplying new blood to a doomed Huddersfield first eleven.

The youngsters revelled in Shankly's coaching methods and gave unstinting obedience to a man whose talents were obvious. Shankly's boys grew from strength to strength in an atmosphere in which their every need was catered for, their future in the game of paramount importance to their mentor.

Inevitably, Huddersfield were relegated at the end of season '55–'56.

The following season started no better – Huddersfield's first team had suffered early defeats in their Division Two campaign which set alarm bells ringing at boardroom level. In direct contrast to this, Shankly's exciting, effervescent reserves had picked up where they had left off, displaying enthusiasm and skills which made watching second-team football a better option than following the first eleven! Indeed, it was said that when first-team players dropped down to the reserves, they had been promoted to Shankly's team!

Smarting at criticism levelled at his tactics, Beattie had, on a couple of occasions, offered his resignation to the board who opted to keep him on in the hope that matters would improve.

In November 1956, however, following a succession of three league defeats, including a 4–1 trouncing by neighbours Sheffield United, Beattie again tendered his resignation. This time the board accepted. Although he and Shankly had their disagreements, Beattie wasted no time in recommending to the board that they could do worse than offer their reserve team coach the manager's post.

Shankly was popular in Huddersfield. He and Ness had made many friends and his acceptance of the offer to manage the club was instant.

Following his appointment on 5 November 1956, Shankly announced to the local press: 'I will work hard for the club but I won't make any predictions. I expect to get 100 per cent effort from the players. I gave that when I was playing and that is all I ask of them . . . I want them all to fight for Huddersfield Town.'

Almost immediately the gloom that had shrouded Leeds Road lifted. Early on, Shankly had impressed the Huddersfield folk and his reputation went before him.

There was an air of expectation that things would get better and that the club would fight its way back to its rightful position in league and cup soccer. After all, hadn't Bill Shankly produced a reserve team ready to display their talents at a higher level?

Initial results were promising; the crowds flocked back. The 16-year-old Denis Law scored his first league goal against Notts County on Boxing Day 1956, while young Dave Hickson was banging them in with great regularity. The youngsters strived hard on Shankly's behalf, always remembering his teachings: 'Assert yourself, play with confidence.' 'Forget your strengths, work on your weaknesses.' The cockiness of the prodigies, however, was not enough to regain First Division status for Huddersfield who could only finish mid-table.

Shankly faced some criticism about initiating his youngsters too quickly into league football. Perhaps they had some growing to do first. His retort was always, 'If you're good enough, you're old enough' – a point of view shared by his friend and fellow countryman Matt Busby at Manchester United, whose coaching methods and philosophy about the game ran parallel to Shankly's.

Shankly had learned a lot from his experiences at Preston, Carlisle, Grimsby and Workington. He knew within himself, however, that he had much more to give as a manager. As with the other clubs, he had a natural distrust of directors and found it a great strain to sit through boardroom meetings. Doing his utmost to avoid desk duties, he would rather busy himself with 'the more important matter of coaching', seeing to the players' needs and attending to the fabric of the stadium.

Not for Shankly the collar-and-tie image his counterparts at other clubs adopted. He was never to be addressed as Mr Shankly by his players. He was one of them: Bill or 'Boss', if you had to, would suffice.

It was during those days at Huddersfield that the great sense of humour, wit and confidence which Shankly had lost a little during the previous three years returned. Players and staff at Huddersfield became more relaxed under their new manager whose leg-pulling and pranks helped ease the tensions felt by players under constant pressure by fans to deliver results. He would chatter incessantly, mostly about football, believing that if his staff were talking, laughing or joking, they wouldn't be worrying about their form or the impending match. 'A happy club,' Shankly would say, 'is a successful club.'

Never one to criticise, Shankly believed that if he was learning his trade – which he maintained he was still in the process of doing – he would be bound to make mistakes. If he erred, he would much rather receive constructive criticism and encouragement than negative chastisement and embarrassment, and if such a philosophy held good for him, then the same would apply to his staff. He never criticised his players openly in public.

The 1958–59 season was to be Shankly's last at Leeds Road. Little did he know that when his 'babes' gave Liverpool FC a 5–0 thrashing that year, he was soon to move on to the dawn of a new era which would live forever in the annals of football history!

That final season saw Huddersfield, again, finish midway in the league. Although his youngsters were shaping up well, Shankly was having trouble holding on to Denis Law, in particular, as the First Division managers hovered. Shankly felt he needed a couple of new faces to bolster his promising young team. Emerging stars Ian St John and Brian Clough, at Motherwell and Middlesbrough, were earmarked as the two who would make his team complete.

Dundee United's giant centre-half Ron Yeats was identified as a rock around which Shankly could mould his 'dream team' of rising starlets. With these men in place, he was on the verge of assembling a quality side, fit to challenge at the highest level.

But Huddersfield board of directors had other ideas. Leeds Road stadium was their biggest asset; they set aside money for stadium upgrading, floodlighting and office refurbishment. Shankly was told to continue grooming his starlets, concentrate his energies on the development of home-grown talent whilst the board would deliver a stadium fit for the best to play or spectate in.

He would also have to accept the selling-on of his best starlets to help finance the general running of the club and the new stadium.

Shankly fought tooth and nail to keep hold of Denis Law, using all his powers of persuasion. But the writing was on the wall.

Huddersfield had been a happy experience for Shankly. Family life had never been better: Ness had settled in the town and Barbara was at a good school. Shankly himself was more relaxed, the consequence of building a promising team. Social outlets included an excellent local cinema, while Shankly thoroughly enjoyed regular Sunday afternoon kick-abouts with the locals on nearby common ground. Glenbuck and Glasgow were within travelling distance. Everyone was content.

Or maybe not. Despite his being in better form, Shankly had again reached a point where the lack of money available to him was frustrating his attempts to build 'the greatest football team ever'. This frustration was, nevertheless, tempered as Shankly constantly reminded himself of the unhappiness suffered by Ness at Grimsby – he had family responsibilities. Perhaps he should narrow his football horizons for the sake of his devoted wife and daughters.

This dilemma, however, was soon to end as fate took a hand in matters.

While Carlisle, Grimsby and Workington were footballing outposts, Huddersfield had provided Shankly with a stage from which his actions could be viewed by the wider soccer audience. He was sought after by bigger fish. Leeds United had sounded out Huddersfield about the possible availability of their manager, but history was about to be written when, following a Huddersfield versus Cardiff match on 17 October 1959, Shankly, who it was known was looking around for another club, was approached by two gentlemen who asked him if he would 'like to become the manager of the best club in the country'.

In his own inimitable style, Shankly quipped; 'Why, is Matt Busby packing it in?'

Smiling, one of the men introduced himself as T.V. Williams, chairman of Liverpool FC. His colleague was Liverpool director Harry Latham.

Tom Williams had spent the whole of the 90 minutes of the Huddersfield versus Cardiff match staring at Shankly. The tracksuited Huddersfield 'gaffer' constantly encouraged his team from the sidelines, argued every refereeing decision and commanded strict obedience from his players as he incessantly barked instructions as to how the match should be played. Hardly off his feet for the full duration of the match, Shankly displayed an energy which impressed the Liverpool supremo who had heard glowing reports about the Scotsman's coaching abilities.

Liverpool had also taken notice of Shankly's communication skills, his ability to weld club and community into one unit. Shankly, they assessed, had the character and charisma to unlock a dormant power and passion harnessed in the hearts of Liverpool supporters.

Liverpool were playing second fiddle to near neighbours Everton who were playing in the First Division, while the Anfield Road Reds were languishing in the Second.

Crowds of around 30,000 were turning up regularly at Anfield only to make the full-time trek home disgruntled and saddened as their favourites tumbled in league and cup matches. Reds supporters had become the brunt of jokes by Evertonians delighted by this turn of events and beside themselves with joy at the ineptitude of their city rivals, which included an FA Cup defeat at the hands of non-league Worcester City.

Liverpool had been a great club. Five League Championships had been won in the past and Anfield idols had included none other than the great Billy Liddell.

T.V. Williams had a hunch that in Shankly there was the potential to both produce quality Liverpool teams and rally the city around the club's endeavours to regain their status as an outfit to be reckoned with at the highest level in the game. How right Williams was. How sound was his assessment of Shankly's potential and capabilities.

The world was about to witness a 'marriage' straight out of heaven! The courtship, though, would have to come first.

12

By the Scruff of the Neck

On being asked about the impact Shankly had during his early years at Anfield, Ron Yeats said: 'He took it by the scruff of the neck and shook it into life.'

Liverpool FC was in a state of chaos when their new manager arrived in 1959. Money was tight and Anfield stadium was in a state of disrepair due to a lack of financial investment as the club slipped further and further into the doldrums.

Crumbling terracing, a lack of proper toilet or refreshment facilities for both players and spectators, a dank and draughty gabled main stand – the new manager did not exactly get the feeling that Liverpool were going places as he parked his Austin A40 behind Anfield stadium on the morning of Monday, 14 December.

Shankly had played at Anfield on several occasions but had not really taken much notice of the disrepair that the famous old stadium had fallen into.

'The place was a dump,' recalled Ness, who had begun to wonder about the wisdom of her husband in bringing the family to such a town which, compared to Huddersfield, was quite uninviting. Liverpool, on first impression, reminded Ness of the gloomier parts of her native Glasgow. She had loved Huddersfield and had not really been keen to move.

Liverpool at this time was moving into financial decline as its importance as a dockside trading centre had diminished. Having been given its City Charter by King John in 1207, Liverpool became a major trading centre, firstly with Ireland. During the eighteenth century, Liverpool Dock had become one of the most important European centres in the slave trading industry. The River Mersey was soon crowded with ships bearing coffee, tea, sugar, chocolate and grain to and from the Americas. Passenger ships carried settlers to Australia, America, India and the Far East whilst emigrants from Russia, Germany and Scandinavia arrived on Merseyside in droves seeking passage to the New World.

The repair and construction of ships became the city's main industry and employer as Liverpool's population expanded. Over half a million Irish immigrants sought shelter and work in the thriving seaport during the Potato Famine of the 1840s, a large Irish colony settling around Liverpool's docklands. Across the Mersey river, the districts of Birkenhead and Wallasey expanded as, by 1900, the Mersey seaport included 40 docks and a thriving shipbuilding industry servicing the needs of the British Empire's sea trade.

Fine town houses, grand ornate shipping and trading company buildings were erected as Victorian Liverpool capitalism boomed. Scots and Welsh families joined the Irish in the search for work in the boom port. Libraries, theatres and civic centres adorned with Gothic architecture were constructed as were roads, tramways and rail-links between the city's districts which housed a workforce earning their daily bread on the Mersey's banks.

The 'Dockers' Umbrella', an overhead railway line running the entire six and a half miles of Merseyside docks, carried workers from Dingle estate in the south to Seaforth docks to the north of the city, workers alighting at 17 stations, one for each dock on the railway's route.

Liverpool was a city not dissimilar to Belfast or Glasgow. The better-off lived in large houses on neat avenues uphill from the bustle of the city and the noise of industry, whilst the labouring classes were huddled together in narrow, terraced, cobbled streets within easy reach of their places of toil.

In the period between the First and Second World War, Liverpool had maintained its importance as a major trading port but, as trading patterns changed during the '50s and '60s, and a move to airfreight and containerisation emerged, the seaport's position in the west of England gave it a distinct disadvantage.

Liverpool's militant trade unionism, born as dockers struggled to defend their jobs and their communities during the periods of recession, gained the port's workers a reputation of being workshy and anarchistic. Liverpudlians were portrayed as being idle and liable to strike at a moment's notice.

This reputation was, of course, exploited to the full by investors and owners who, having earned vast fortunes off the backs of industrious Liverpool workers, had their eyes fixed on other seaports closer to the new European trading nations.

When the Shanklys arrived, shipbuilding and engineering were still providing, albeit contracted, employment opportunities for Liverpool's workforce. Birkenhead had won the order to construct the first Polaris submarines whilst the city fathers were locked into negotiations which would bring the Ford Motor Company to Halewood industrial site.

Ships continued to navigate the Mersey. Liners and cargo vessels ensured that some work was still available for the stevedores, chandlers and crane operators. Many Scousers found employment as deckhands or stewards on luxury cruise ships. The port's decline, though, was there for all to see.

The famous city landmark, the 'Dockers' Umbrella', was dismantled as the number of docks decreased. Warehouses were lying empty as unemployment and its associated spin-offs of crime and juvenile delinquency began to rise.

The city's football clubs, Liverpool and Everton, had become just as depressed. Although Everton had maintained their First Division status and were known as a skilful soccer side, they had failed to win either the League or FA Cup since the war under the management of former Manchester United ace, Johnny Carey.

Across Stanley Park, Liverpool FC had been languishing in the Second Division for four years when Shankly took the helm. Under Shankly's predecessor Phil Taylor, Liverpool had become known as a team who could win or draw a number of home games but who were hopeless away. They were so inconsistent that they were unable to mount any serious challenge for promotion.

In season 1959–60, their first 17 games produced only as many points. Taylor, who was a manager of the old school, had nothing more to offer Liverpool's directors who felt his technique and man-management skills were not sufficient to stop the rot.

Those who know the city of Liverpool will be aware of the fierce rivalry that exists between the two football clubs separated by Stanley Park. This inter-club rivalry is only equalled by the fans of Rangers and Celtic, although Liverpool football fanatics are not divided by the religious bigotry associated with Glasgow's two main rivals.

Tom Williams was only too aware that the 30,000 fans who rolled up to Anfield would soon dwindle if Second Division football continued to be the fare for much longer. Money was getting scarce, more and more fans were being made redundant, and both clubs were vying to attract those who could still afford entrance to games.

First Division tussles at Goodison were better value for money than what was on offer at Anfield. Liverpool FC had to mount a serious challenge for the allegiance of the footballing public. They had been a great club; Williams felt they could be so again. He consulted top football coaches, including Walter Winterbottom, who informed him that the new-style 'tracksuit manager', an ex-player with coaching abilities, was what was required at Anfield. Other experts agreed that Huddersfield's Bill Shankly could be just the man. Shankly's management style, his ability to win over the hearts and minds of players and fans, could be just the tonic needed to lift the sleeping Anfield giant out of its mediocrity.

How prophetic this advice was to be!

During his early negotiations with the Anfield board, Shankly, aware from past experience that his fervour, passion and unlimited energy were not enough if money wasn't available, wrung several concessions, including his overall control of the playing side of operations. This included team selection, coaching requirements, scouting for new talent, training methods and all negotiations in the transfer market.

Prior to Shankly's arrival, Liverpool's directors had enjoyed sole discretion as to which players left or arrived at Anfield.

Shankly never doubted his own ability to earn the £2,500 annual salary he was to be paid. He knew how desperately the Anfield club and its supporters wanted First Division football and was himself inspired by a comment from Ness who, although unsure about living in Liverpool, supported the man she loved in typical style by telling him: 'If you want to realise your ambition of managing in England's top league – Liverpool is your best chance yet.'

Assembling Liverpool's press on his appointment, Shankly announced to the city: 'I am very pleased and proud to have been chosen as manager of Liverpool FC – a club with so much great potential. It is my opinion that Liverpool have a crowd of followers which ranks about the greatest in the game. They deserve success – and I hope to be able to do something to help them achieve it. I make no promises except that I shall put everything I have into this job I have so willingly undertaken.'

Veteran Anfield supporter Tommy Solomon recalled that this opening statement from the Reds' new manager inspired the faithful.

'We were struggling in the darkness when, suddenly, this confident, self-assured Scot arrived, giving us a commitment that he would throw his heart and soul into putting the smiles back on our faces. We believed him. We had to!'

Shankly was only too aware of the hardships being faced by Liverpudlians struggling through economic decline. He had himself experienced this back in Glenbuck. When the mill and coal owners were done with you, off they went, leaving communities scraping by for a living until those communities lost their souls and died. Whilst the situation in Liverpool was not as dire as it was in Glenbuck, Shankly had empathy with the feelings of uncertainty many Scousers harboured. He had an affinity with a working class who were feeling insecure, and was only too aware of the importance that football had in their lives. These people needed the feeling of belonging, which allegiance to their football club provided: they needed to know that they were not alone.

This need was met through standing on the terracing with their 'extended family' where, on match-day, they could experience all the drama, excitement, humour and entertainment required to recharge their batteries in order to meet the week-long struggles which lay ahead. Hope in their hearts for the fortunes of their club helped banish despair.

A club such as Liverpool had a duty, an obligation to these people – a class which had helped build the Empire, fought Britain's wars and were struggling to retain their dignity despite uncertainty and adversity.

Shankly would set to work bringing about changes at Anfield 'which would give these great people the greatest team in the world'. Shankly's 'socialism' would be manifested through the 'People's Republic of Anfield' with its own 'Red Army'. A new 'revolution' was about to take place.

One of Shankly's first tasks as manager at Anfield was to appraise the staff complement. In those days, Liverpool staff consisted of a receptionist/secretary, one or two clerical assistants, some part-time cleaning staff, a groundsman and turnstile operators. A few volunteer fans and ex-players would regularly turn up to lend a hand with the odd jobs always required around the creaking stadium.

The club's coaching staff consisted of Bob Paisley, an ex-player in similar mould to Shankly who had played over 250 times for Liverpool between 1939 and 1954. Joe Fagan was a home-bred Scouser who had played at Manchester City, Bradford and Rochdale before returning to his native city in 1958 as a member of Anfield's coaching team. The third Anfield coach was Reuben Bennett, a Scot who had played with Hull City, Queen of the South and Dundee prior to coaching Ayr United, Motherwell and Third Lanark. This coaching threesome were a bit apprehensive at their first meeting with Shankly. Both Paisley and Fagan had played against him on several occasions and knew Shankly to be a stubborn, hard-headed Ayrshireman. It was reported that he could be hard to work with, sometimes arrogant, mostly uncompromising in his views. And he had that James Cagney swagger!

Shankly called his three coaches together and announced: 'You fellows have been here, some of you, a long time. I have my own training system and will work in co-operation with you. I will lay down the plans and, gradually, we will be on the same wavelength. I want one thing – I want loyalty. I don't want anybody to carry stories about anyone else . . . I want everyone to be loyal to each other. Everything we do will be for Liverpool FC – that makes strength.'

Shankly needn't have worried. Paisley, Fagan and Bennett were already on his wavelength. Their outlook on the game was the same as the new manager; they simply needed a leader worthy of their collective respect and with the man-management skills to maximise their collective talents. Shankly was to prove to be just that leader.

Paisley and Shankly hit it off from the word go. 'Gunner' Paisley, as he was known, due to his war service in Europe and the Western Desert, had been a similar type of player to his new boss and had the same philosophy on football.

'He was a team man, totally dedicated to football and, in particular, Liverpool FC,' Shankly later said of Paisley.

Like Shankly, Paisley was a battler. A canny Geordie, he had a sense of humour and wit as sharp as his Scottish manager. Indeed, he welcomed the new leadership which would allow his own visions to flourish.

Of Shankly he said: 'There was no way you could not work for him . . . You can sense when people have a bit of respect for you and you could feel that Bill had that respect for us and we for him – it was as simple as that – respect!'

Here was the perfect football marriage of manager and trusted assistant. Shankly and Paisley were described by veteran supporters as 'soul-mates just waiting to meet each other'.

Nevertheless, Shankly made no bones about it: he was the boss. Team captain Ronnie Moran was also taken quickly into the new manager's confidence and recalled later: 'I learned more in the first three months with Shankly than I had in the past seven years as a pro. I wished I had been five years younger.'

Another figure who made up Shankly's 'team' was Albert Shelley. Officially retired, Shelley was a handyman who had found it difficult to leave Anfield. He was always around the place doing little painting jobs, cleaning the changing-rooms, or attending to small repairs. Shankly admired the man's refusal to fade away into retirement and his obvious commitment to the club, so he invited him to become an official part of the new Anfield regime – an invitation which Shelley gratefully accepted.

Troops mustered, Shankly set about the job. Again, as with his previous management roles, he involved himself in every aspect of the club. He secured a house for the family close to Liverpool's Melwood training ground in the city's West Derby district – the same house in which Ness lives today.

Melwood training ground was in a shocking state. Resembling more a rundown village cricket green than a professional football club's coaching facility, the pitch had no watering system and the old pavilion was in dire need of repair and a good lick of paint.

The training pitch was rutted, bare and bumpy. Where grass did grow, it was untended and weed infested. Shankly remarked that the club's training ground was 'of more use to locals exercising their dogs than it was to a club exercising its playing staff'.

Liverpool not only needed new players, they required a decent training ground for fitness and coaching purposes, not to mention a stadium fit for the promotion to First Division football which was being planned.

Although a little despondent and reflecting on the wisdom of his move to Anfield, Shankly felt that the club's potential was enormous. They had a major asset no other British club possessed – the fans! Certainly, Liverpool was facing something of an economic crisis. The war was much to blame for the fact that the team was rundown and the stadium a shambles, but all of this could change.

If he could convince the Liverpool directors to give him full rein and make finance available to him, there was absolutely nothing to stop him turning this whole business around.

Ness was right: he *could* take Liverpool into the First Division. The city was buzzing with expectation; there existed a power in Liverpool which was yet to be unleashed. Shankly felt that the city of Liverpool was poised to rise Phoenix-like and meet the challenge of the new era– Liverpool FC could, and should, be part of that rising!

Former player, now public relations officer at Anfield, Brian Hall recalled: 'Things were beginning to happen in Liverpool. The city was becoming the place to be in. Liverpool was on the verge of becoming the centre for the arts, poetry, pop and rock music. Although the old city of shipbuilding and merchant trade was disappearing, a new Liverpool was being born through the university, the beat clubs, the artists' and writers' colonies – The Beatles and Beatlemania which would rock the world were just around the corner. Shankly and Liverpool FC came together at a time of change. Liverpudlians would have the Beatles, the arts, the actors and writers who would bring new prestige to their city – they also wanted a great football team so they could show the rest of England that, far from being finished, their city was reborn and could produce the best in culture, art, prose, poetry – and the people's game.'

Shankly would assist Liverpool in once more raising the proud wings of the Liver Bird.

13

Laying the Foundations

Shankly used the 1959–60 season to evaluate his playing complement. There were a few good players around such as Roger Hunt, Ron Moran, Gerry Byrne and Jimmy Melia. Scotland's international goalkeeper Tommy Younger was at Anfield when Shankly arrived, as was another ex-Hibernian Scot, Jimmy Harrower.

Phil Taylor had signed Everton's popular goalscorer Dave Hickson, whilst the legendary Billy Liddell was reaching the twilight of his career.

Of 40 players on the club's books, Shankly estimated that many were past their best. Although many of the playing staff felt an immediate clear-out was on the cards, Shankly took time to move players on and convince them, where necessary, that it was time to pack it in.

Shankly's sensitivity, his awareness of what it meant to a man to be told his services were no longer required, led to this weeding-out process becoming a little protracted. He would find players other clubs or alternative employment rather than just see them out the door.

Under the new regime, Liverpool finished the 1959–60 league campaign in third position. That and the following season were periods of transition as Shankly laid the foundation for promotion to the First Division.

The Shankly road to success, however, would have to be argued first of all in the Anfield boardroom. Shankly's plan of action was to use the coming season preparing for the elevation of Liverpool FC to top league status. He explained to his coaching team and the fans that this process could take a season or two as 'there is so much to be done'. New players were needed, the club's coaching and training facilities required upgrading and Anfield stadium would need to be brought up to a suitable standard for First Division teams and supporters.

Leading a workforce of staff, players and supporters, Shankly began his own 'long march'. Repairs were carried out on Melwood and Anfield as his volunteer carpenters, painters, odd-job men, plumbers and landscapers set about renovating both stadium and training ground. Working day and night coaching his players, seeing to the daily running of the club and supervising his building squads, Shankly exhausted himself. He kept going, though, as the words of encouragement from Ness rang in his ears: 'If you want to manage in the First Division, Liverpool are your best bet!'

Liverpool fans were impressed by the enthusiasm of the club's new manager but the pragmatic Scousers knew that all of this huff and puff around Anfield and Melwood meant little if new players were not to appear soon.

Leading a band of recruits in improvements was one thing, but where was the team to bring glory days back to Anfield?

Over at Everton they had bought in quality players such as Alex Young and George Thomson from Heart of Midlothian. Billy Bingham, Alex Parker and Roy Vernon had joined the Blues' ranks as John Moores, boss of Littlewoods Pools had made tens of thousands of pounds available to the Goodison Park management. With players like these at Everton, the Liverpool fans could envisage years of the Reds playing second fiddle to their arch rivals. Shankly was acutely aware of the fans' feelings.

He had been promised £60,000 to spend on players on his appointment but had seen little of it. Early attempts by

Shankly to bring Denis Law over from Huddersfield and Jack Charlton from Leeds United were thwarted by the board. Gates began to fall as Anfield fans became disenchanted with their manager's obvious inability to persuade the board to part with transfer money. Noticing the ever-increasing gaps in the terracing, Anfield's directors asked Shankly what the problem was.

'The problem,' he replied, 'is that I want the club in the First Division and to do that I need money to buy players.'

Shankly's frustration and anger towards the Liverpool board almost reached breaking point as the directors began to involve themselves in team selections. Things reached boiling point as promising young Liverpool outside left, Johnny Morrissey, was sold to Everton under Shankly's nose in a hushed-up deal.

The directors had gone back on their initial promises. They had agreed to make money available for players; they had agreed to leave team selection to the manager and had given him sole discretion in the transfer market; all of these promises had been broken.

Liverpool had, again, finished third in Division Two at the end of season 1960–61. Shankly had become depressed at the situation at Anfield. In the factories and pubs of Liverpool the talk was of the Scots manager's obvious lack of qualifications and ability. Had they been sold a pig in a poke? After all, he had never really been involved in top-flight soccer. At this juncture, lesser men than Shankly would have called it a day. Old friend Matt Busby coaxed his fellow countryman into staying at Anfield, perhaps giving it another season or two to see how things would work out.

During the summer of 1961, events took a turn. Littlewoods boss John Moores had for several years been a shareholder at both Everton and Liverpool Football Clubs. During 1960 he became more interested in events at Goodison Park, throwing his efforts and cash into the Blues' revival whilst maintaining a lesser interest in affairs at Anfield.

A close friend of T.V. Williams, Moores was becoming

anxious at reports from his associate of the rift between Shankly and Liverpool board members. Although he had opted to throw his weight behind Everton, Moores was aware of his responsibility to the other half of the football-mad city he dearly loved. Liverpool FC's finances were in a mess. Gates were dropping dramatically, and supporters were losing faith in their manager whom Williams felt was the man for the job, if only he had the finances to commence team building.

A solution was found. Littlewoods chief accountant and finance executive Eric Sawyer was persuaded by Moores to join the Liverpool board of directors. Sawyer knew nothing about football but, as finance chief of the multi-million-pound Littlewoods empire, he knew plenty about financial investment.

Sawyer's brief from Moores was to assess and evaluate the state of Liverpool FC's finances and, if possible, 'turn the business round'.

Initially, Shankly felt that Sawyer's presence on the Liverpool board would make little difference. He had seen directors come and go before. Lawyers, accountants, bankers, tradesmen, politicians – it didn't matter what they were, none of them had been able to offer any form of tangible help.

Sawyer, though, was a different proposition as Shankly was soon to discover. The encounter between Shankly and Sawyer was to prove the foundation for the beginning of a fantastic adventure which would bring greatness to Liverpool FC and immortality for the manager, who would be given the backing to deliver his promise to the Anfield Red-necks.

He would build 'the greatest team in the world for the greatest fans in the world'.

Eric Sawyer may have known little about football, but he certainly proved to be an astute judge of character. Almost immediately he identified Liverpool FC's greatest asset and development potential to be in the club manager's driving ambition, his zest for life and grasp of what was required to make Liverpool FC a vibrant force.

Sawyer quickly assessed Shankly's strengths and came to the conclusion that if this man were given control then things could begin to happen around the slumbering Anfield. Impressed at the loyalty given to Shankly by his coaching staff, the accountant was won over to the argument that those who knew football should run football, and those who knew money should provide that commodity where investment would bring results.

Shankly and Sawyer spent days discussing the manager's philosophy on football, his training and coaching methods, and the value of the supporter to the club.

Both men shared a common goal: Sawyer wanted Liverpool to become a successful business; Shankly aspired to making Liverpool the most successful soccer team in England – and beyond.

Sawyer saw both as synonymous with each other and declared to Shankly: 'You find the players to build this great team, I'll find the money.'

Shankly was overjoyed. In the face of adversity he had found an ally, someone with the intelligence and business acumen with whom he could share his vision.

Liverpool FC could become the proud representatives of this great city as it moved into the new era of the '60s and '70s. It could be done: all that was required was a board which had the guts to invest for the future. A delighted Shankly felt that Sawyer could be just that man to inject a little gumption, a little confidence, into the Liverpool boardroom.

This Sawyer did. He convinced fellow directors that, in Shankly, they had a specialist, a professional, whose management skills and coaching techniques, tactical awareness and ability to command respect from players were invaluable assets to the club.

Sawyer insisted that if Liverpool FC were to be run properly as a business, as a football club facing up to the challenges of a new Britain, then only the best would do. He convinced the board that Shankly had been pointing the way forward – players and fans should have the best of everything, Anfield should be reconstructed to provide a stadium fit for the new dawn.

Most importantly, Shankly should have at his disposal the

best coaching and training facilities and financial resources to encourage the best footballers to Anfield.

If these terms were not agreeable then surely board members would have to give account to both investors and the Liverpool population, who were watching with bated breath as Sawyer and Shankly attempted to spark their Anfield revolution.

Fortunately, Sawyer and Shankly won the day, and from then on Liverpool FC were in the business of providing only the best – for the best.

As Shankly was to recall later: 'Eric Sawyer was the beginning of Liverpool.'

Shankly felt a great weight lift from his shoulders. At last he was free to concentrate all his energies into building the greatest team ever. He could now look the Anfield fans in the eye and say: 'Here we go!'

14

Up We Go

Towards the end of the 1960–61 season Shankly was relaxing at home over Sunday breakfast reading his edition of the Sunday Post. Glancing through the Scottish football results, he noticed that Motherwell's Ian St John was unsettled at Fir Park. The dazzling Scottish striker had been attracting the interest of several English clubs, including Newcastle United, and was keen to move. The abolition of the maximum wage meant that big money could be earned with the top English sides. St John had attracted Shankly's attention three years before when he unsuccessfully attempted to sign him for Huddersfield. His impending availability rekindled that interest. A Scottish Under-23 cap, St John, at 5ft 8in, wasn't the tallest of centre forwards, but he had pace, great shooting ability, fantastic ball control and could head a ball better than most.

The asking price for St John was quoted at around £35,000. Shankly immediately contacted Motherwell, informing them of Liverpool's interest in the centre forward and arranged to visit Fir Park the following day for talks.

A quick telephone call to Eric Sawyer followed, Shankly informing him that 'the best centre forward in Scotland' was for sale. The player, St John, was the very centre-forward

Liverpool were seeking to partner Roger Hunt. Sawyer trusted Shankly's assessment of St John, telling the manager to go ahead with his full backing.

Next day, Shankly and T.V. Williams travelled to Motherwell to watch St John play in a local derby game against Hamilton Academical. Following negotiations with both the Motherwell directors and St John, the classy Scots centre-forward was Anfield bound on Tuesday, 2 May 1961 for a fee of £37,500. As negotiations over St John's transfer were taking place, one or two Liverpool board members, aghast at such a fortune being spent, wondered whether Liverpool could really afford to sign the player. 'We can't afford not to sign him!' retorted Sawyer.

St John's debut for Liverpool a week later saw the new centre score three goals in a 4–3 defeat by Everton in the Liverpool Senior Cup final. Liverpool fans in the capacity 50,000 crowd at Goodison Park were ecstatic. The display by St John – man of the match – was far above that of Everton's glittering array of stars.

Another significant signing took place that season. Shankly had worked out his blueprint for a successful Liverpool team. A great striker, a towering centre-half and a first-class goalkeeper would give him the 'backbone' around which to assemble his squad.

Dundee United's giant centre-half Ron Yeats had also attracted Shankly's attention in the Huddersfield days. A National Serviceman, Yeats was quite happy at Tannadice travelling to and from his northern homeland from a posting in the south of England.

Dundee United were an attractive side and were playing well in the Scottish First Division following recent promotion. Jerry Kerr's youngsters were happy at Tannadice and United were reluctant to part with any of their staff.

In June 1961, Liverpool tabled an offer of £20,000 for Yeats's signature only to be informed that a figure nearer £40,000 was required for the transfer of the 6ft 3in centre-half. Liverpool were reluctant to go over £20,000, given the money recently spent on St John. Shankly, though, persisted in his interest. Sawyer agreed that Yeats should become a Liverpool player but said to the manager: 'Wait a bit then we'll make them an offer they can't refuse.'

On Saturday, 22 July, T.V. Williams and Shankly met with Dundee United officials and Yeats in Edinburgh's North British Hotel where a final bid of £30,000, secured by Sawyer from the board, was offered for Yeats's transfer.

Of that day Ron Yeats recalled: 'We were standing in the hotel foyer and Shankly kept circling around me, looking me up and down. I felt like a slave at auction. I was craning my neck round to see what he was doing at my back when Shankly suddenly snapped. "Christ, son, you must be over seven feet tall!" I replied, "No, I'm only six foot three." Shankly replied, "Well, son, when you turn out for Liverpool you'll be seven feet tall."'

Yeats wasn't all that convinced that Liverpool was where he wanted to go. He was happy at United. 'I asked Mr Shankly where Liverpool was, as I didn't really know what part of England it was in.'

'We're in the First Division, son,' was the reply.

'That's not true,' said Yeats.

'Ah, but son,' Shankly informed him, 'we soon will be with you in the team.'

'You couldn't turn the man down,' Yeats recalled. 'He convinced me that I would be joining the greatest club in the world – I had to go.'

The signing of St John and Yeats were master strokes. Liverpool's new team also included goalkeeper Bert Slater, Ian Callaghan, Gerry Byrne, Alan A'Court, Roger Hunt, Tommy Leishman and Ronnie Moran. Anfield fans were delirious as the Hunt–St John partnership thrived in a season where nearly 100 goals were scored.

The defence was almost impregnable with Ron Yeats towering like a Colossus at centre-back. As average home gates swelled to 50,000, Liverpool amassed 62 out of a possible 84 league points and won the 1961–62 Second Division championship.

The Kop end of Anfield, the large bank of terracing which

held 24,000 fans, was packed to capacity for each home game during that '61–'62 season. The smiles had returned to the faces of the faithful. Kop-ites were extremely vociferous in support of their favourites, taking two popular hit-tunes of the day and adapting them to become anthems. The noisy Liverpool Kop intimidated visiting teams and was said to be worth a one-goal start – at least to a Liverpool side which Ron Yeats recalled 'had an extra man in every home game due to the Kop'.

Promotion to the First Division was won on Saturday, 21 April 1962. Five league matches were still remaining as Liverpool clinched the Second Division title in front of a packed 50,000 crowd, defeating visitors Southampton 2–0.

This was the moment Shankly had been waiting for. Ness was right; he would manage in the First Division with Liverpool.

The Kop was jubilant. The covered, steep-banked terracing reverberated to the sound of the choir who sang themselves hoarse in appreciation of their team's achievement.

'People forget,' said Tommy Solomon. 'Liverpool actually has three cathedrals – the Cathedral, Paddy's Wigwam and the Kop!'

For years the famous Anfield Kop, arguably housing the most fanatical fans in Europe, had been silent as Liverpool struggled in Division Two. Now, thanks to the foresight of Tom Williams, the craft of Shankly, and the intervention of Eric Sawyer, the voice of the people was again soaring above the stadium and beyond.

The crowds refused to spill out into Walton Breck Road following that title-clinching match until Shankly and the players returned to receive their just accolades.

'We want Shankly! We want the Reds!' chanted a delirious Anfield crowd, swaying and singing in the April rain until, eventually, to tumultuous applause, Shankly and Williams reappeared in the directors' box to return the crowd's salutes. It was announced that the players were in the bath but this did nothing to silence the jubilant crowd who continued chanting until, amid the most fantastic crowd scenes and deafening noise, the players reappeared on the pitch in various states of undress.

'They had to come out, otherwise we'd have stayed until the next Saturday,' said veteran fan Ted Brooks.

Pandemonium ensued. Both Ian St John and Ron Yeats disappeared into the crowd, eventually having to be rescued by police.

Yeats recalled: 'It was the most frightening thing I'd ever seen.'

It was several hours before the Anfield area was eventually cleared of celebrating fans. The rafters of The Albert pub next to the stadium shook as the Anfield faithful celebrated in style. Merseyside was filled with pride at the fact that both city teams were playing in the First Division again at last.

On Monday morning, the crowds couldn't help but reflect on the talent oozing out of the city . . .

The London sound of the Dave Clark Five or the beat music of Manchester and Newcastle groups had nothing on Liverpool's Beatles; the southerners could claim their Rolling Stones but nothing compared with the Mersey sound.

Frankie Vaughan, Cilla Black, Gerry and the Pacemakers, The Merseybeats.

Weren't Liverpool's comedians the best? Just look at rising stars Tarbuck, Dodd and company. Now the city had two football teams playing at the highest level in the English game!

The telegrams of congratulations poured into Anfield from the great and the good. Actress Rita Tushingham was 'proud of my city'; MPs, businessmen and local politicians all welcomed Liverpool FC's contribution in portraying the city as a place where success could be achieved.

Liverpool was set to take England and the world by storm. Little did the Scousers know just how big an impact Liverpool FC, the Mersey sound and the new wave of culture were to have on their lives.

Bill Shankly did! He was, after all, a man of vision. There was nothing the people of this great city could not achieve. All they needed was the confidence to step out and say 'we are the greatest people in the world'.

Shankly wasn't satisfied with mere promotion to the First Division. When the directors presented the Anfield staff with silver cigarette boxes to mark the achievement he quipped: 'You're not satisfied with that, are you? Next time we come back for the presents, we will have won the big league – the First Division!'

Shankly spent the close-season encouraging fans to shout that their club was the greatest in the world. He would enter the First Division backed by a city and a following whose passionate loyalty towards their football team would cause panic among the players and supporters of lesser towns and cities.

Visiting Fortress Anfield would become a daunting prospect to even the most seasoned football campaigners. He told supporters: 'We're not going there to make up the numbers – we're going to make the division title our property.'

This prophecy would indeed materialise in the not too distant future.

15

'We Love You, Yeah, Yeah, Yeah'

Season 1962–63 provided a learning experience for Shankly's young Division Two champions. The English First Division at that time was chock-full of gifted, talented players turning out for teams such as Manchester United, Arsenal, Tottenham Hotspur, Chelsea, Leeds United and, of course, the high-flying Everton side. It was one thing to dominate the Second Division, quite another to storm past teams containing the likes of Dave Mackay, the Charltons, Norman Hunter, Alex Young and company.

This was a league of hard tackling, no-nonsense backs and sharp, speedy forwards. A league packed with international stars and giants of the game. Shankly's young pretenders to the throne would have a road to travel yet before their apprenticeships were fully served.

New signings, however, would add to the team's strength. Willie Stevenson, a classy midfielder, was bought from Glasgow Rangers for £20,000, while Jim Furnell, a promising goalkeeper bought from Burnley in 1961 for £18,000, would prove a reliable last line of defence until young Tommy Lawrence was ready to make the step up from reserve to first-team football.

Most football teams who go through a league programme

experiencing only rare defeats suffer a crisis of confidence when, on promotion to a higher division, they discover victories are not so easy to come by. Liverpool were no different. Players, almost unaccustomed to defeat, became upset as Liverpool suffered an anxious introduction to football 'upstairs'.

Finishing eighth at the end of the season, the Anfield side had, nevertheless, acquitted themselves well. Uncertainty and lack of confidence at the start of the season resulted in lost points which could have been won by a team playing attractive, controlled football, had they settled to their new environment sooner.

However, a stirring run in the FA Cup had raised the Anfield fans' hopes of glory in successive years. Disposing of Wrexham, Barnsley, Arsenal and West Ham on the FA Cup trail, Liverpool lined up against Leicester City in the semifinal at Hillsborough. Playing Leicester off the park, Liverpool's luck was out as they slipped to a 1–0 defeat. All things considered, the season had gone well. Shankly was convinced his team could match anyone in the First Division. He had assembled a good squad who knew at the end of season '62–'63 just what would be expected of them the following season.

Everton had won the title that season. Shankly was determined that the Liverpool faithful who had packed Anfield to capacity at home games and travelled in their legions to away fixtures would have the last laugh on their rivals next time round.

As Liverpool prepared for their second assault on the First Division title, Shankly brought in another player, Peter Thompson from Preston. Thompson recalled Shankly telling him on his arrival at Anfield: 'Son, I'm going to make you the greatest player of all time. You'll be so fast you'll be able to catch pigeons.'

Thompson was a skilful left-winger who quickly won the hearts of the Kop faithful with dazzling displays that reminded old-timers of the likes of Finney and Matthews.

Shankly was ready. His players were fit in mind and body. He felt confident that his boys would rise to the occasion as they did on their first two outings of the new season when they defeated Chelsea and Wolves, both away from home. Confidence waned a bit, however, as players began to slip up in home games. Playing First Division football in front of the Kop had become a problem for a few of the team. Calling his players together, Shankly asked them what was wrong.

The players replied that due to pressure from home support, they were trying too hard and not playing the relaxed, confident soccer which was bringing away victories.

Shankly applied his psychology to each member of the team. At training sessions and in pre-match chats he would tell them that they were the greatest players in England. If they weren't, they wouldn't be at Anfield.

Players were continually bombarded with compliments about their abilities until, on the tenth game of the season, they met champions and arch-rivals Everton at Anfield.

A dazzling Liverpool performance produced a 2–1 victory over the Blues. This defeat of Everton with their glittering array of talent was the perfect tonic. The Red Army began its march to victory. With St John, Hunt and Thompson in devastating form, four-, five- and six-goal thrashings were regularly handed out to opponents who found themselves reeling at Liverpool's pace and stamina.

'We were the fittest team in the country,' recalled Roger Hunt.

Indeed, Liverpool's incredible fitness was a major factor in the league title run-in. Team spirit was also of the essence. Shankly's philosophy was, 'If you had good players, each playing his heart out for his team-mates and the jersey, you were well on the way.'

Looking back, Ron Yeats said: 'We weren't brilliant. We were a bunch of very good players, carefully gelled together by Shankly. He shaped our style of play, built up each individual's confidence and had us so match-fit each week it was frightening.'

Shankly's tactic of rubbishing opponents contributed

greatly to his team's championship winning year. London teams were a bunch of 'soft southerners'; opposition goal-keepers were 'past it'; rival centre-forwards 'couldn't score in a darts match'.

As the season's end approached, Liverpool players believed they were invincible. A 5–0 drubbing of Arsenal in front of a 50,000 capacity crowd secured the First Division championship title.

'We love you, yeah, yeah, yeah,' sang the packed Kop, most of whom had queued outside Anfield overnight to be sure of getting in the following day.

The players responded with a lap of honour, carrying a mock league championship trophy: outgoing champions Everton had not delivered the real silverware in time for a presentation on the final whistle at Anfield!

Shankly said: 'This is the greatest moment of my footballing life.'

Sawyer and Shankly would have afforded each other a quiet wink as Liverpool's board of directors patted each other on the back and joined in the celebrations which followed the '63–'64 First Division championship victory.

They had both been proved correct in their assessment of what it would take to get to this position.

Shankly and his backroom boys had assembled a formidable football team; Sawyer had seen to it that the finance was available to carry out this development which, in turn, brought tremendous revenues through the gates. The Shankly–Sawyer partnership had been instrumental in giving birth to a Liverpool dynasty which would go on to deliver pleasure and entertainment to thousands upon thousands of Liverpudlian citizens, and exiles, for years to come. That's what the game was all about.

When the championship trophy was eventually handed over by Everton, Shankly held it aloft for press pictures saying: 'I came, I saw, I conquered.' Glenbuck would have forgiven their son for this momentary lapse of humility. He had worked hard for that day and was entitled to bask a little in the glory.

As all Liverpool partied for weeks following the great championship win, English football agreed that Liverpool were, indeed, worthy ambassadors in the coming European Cup campaign.

Merseyside couldn't get the close-season over quickly enough. The prospect of Liverpool and Everton fighting it out for league supremacy; European football nights at Anfield; and, who knows, perhaps the FA Cup would be paraded along Lime Street.

16

Wembley and Europe

As the First Division championship trophy was placed in the Anfield Trophy Room for the first time in 17 years, Shankly began to prepare his squad for the challenge of the 1964–65 season.

It wasn't going to be easy. Liverpool would be battling on three fronts: to retain their league title, wage a European Cup campaign and make a bid for FA Cup glory.

As the Reds were put through their paces prior to the season's kick-off, Shankly knew that all his powers of persuasion would be required if his boys were to embrace the challenge in all three trophies.

A meeting of his coaching colleagues was called to assess the current playing staff, to see whether new blood may be required in order to bolster the squad for the coming forays.

Shankly would meet with Paisley, Fagan and Bennett in a little office under the Anfield stand which was called the boot room. This little room, containing hampers, kit and spare boots, was a quiet place where Shankly and his staff could lock themselves in and discuss nothing but football. The boot room was a sort of sacred place where entry was by invitation only, an inner sanctum often described as 'the nerve centre of Liverpool FC'.

Shankly and his staff knew that the distraction of the European Cup would have an effect on the coming league and Cup campaigns but felt they had a squad capable of giving a good show in all three competitions. One or two additions could be made to cover for injuries. Young teenage defender Tommy Smith was ready to break through; a couple of players were being sounded out; Tommy Lawrence had taken over in goal. Manchester United reserve striker Phil Chisnall was purchased for £25,000, whilst Jimmy Melia would move on to Wolverhampton Wanderers and Alan A'Court to Tranmere Rovers.

Peter Thompson recalled the famous 'horse' discussion he had with Shankly when at a team talk, and it is reported here:

Shankly: 'You're not listening to me, Thommo. You're so fast, Thommo, you're like a racehorse.'

Thompson: 'Yes, Boss. I'm pretty fast.'

Shankly: 'You're also like a cart-horse. You've so much stamina you can run all day.'

Thompson: 'Yes, Boss. I'm pretty strong.'

Shankly: 'You're also like a hobby-horse. You've no bloody brains!'

Thompson and other players were always under pressure from fans who would ask: 'When are we going to win the FA Cup?'

Liverpudlians had a great desire to travel down to London, take over Wembley and lift the glittering FA trophy from under the noses of 'those soft southerners'. An FA Cup victory in London would settle the North versus South debate. Liverpool were League Champions, Merseyside was better than London when it came to music and the arts – why not really show them by singing 'Ee-aye-addio' as the Reds lifted the Cup?

Shankly knew of this pressure upon his players. As he had feared, Liverpool's league campaign suffered due to the pressure of the European and FA Cup campaigns, but the Anfield faithful enjoyed every minute of it.

European ties and FA Cup encounters were not occasions in which to blood youngsters. If reserves were to be used, these would be mainly in league games. As a result of the number of important fixtures Liverpool had to play, the league campaign fizzled out as Liverpool's Red Army marched on in the cup competitions. Liverpool finished seventh in the league that season but Shankly promised the fans that the following year a 'campaign would be launched to regain the championship'.

The 1964–65 European Cup campaign began with a relatively easy tie against Icelanders Reykjavik who were disposed of by 11 goals to one over the two legs. Ron Yeats tells a great Shankly story surrounding Liverpool's away trip to Iceland.

The journey to Reykjavik proved to be quite a marathon. Liverpool had to travel to Prestwick to catch a plane to Iceland. With some hours to spare before the flight departure, Shankly took his boys on a coach trip of the area.

'We piled into the bus and off we went. Shankly decided to give us a relaxing hour at Butlin's holiday camp. When the bus arrived at Butlin's, the Boss got out and announced to the gateman: "We are Liverpool FC and we're on our way to play a European Cup-tie in Iceland."

'The boys rolled about in fits of laughter as the Ayrshire gateman looked at Shankly and said: "Oh, aye! Well you're on the wrong road, pal, this is Ayr!"'

Following Reykjavik, Liverpool faced Belgian champions Anderlecht, a quality team packed with international players.

A few days before the Anderlecht tie Shankly decided on changing the team strip. Ian St John and Ron Yeats recalled the story.

Shankly told them: 'I thought we might try playing in red shorts, it'll make us even more frightening.' He threw the red shorts to Yeats: 'Try them on.'

Shankly was beside himself at the sight of towering 6ft 3in Yeats in the all-red kit.

'Christ, he looks like a giant. He's frightening, isn't he, Ian?' he asked St John, who then suggested going all the way with red socks.

With Yeats attired in the new all-red strip, Shankly muttered: 'Perfect, just perfect. We'll frighten the hell out of them.'

Shankly's idea was to emulate the all-white Real Madrid strip which gave the Spaniards a distinct psychological advantage over opponents.

Liverpool did indeed look fierce in the new all-red strip. This ferocity was added to as the swaying, roaring Kop urged their heroes on to a 2–0 victory.

Liverpool won the return leg in Brussels 1–0 and qualified to meet West German champions FC Cologne in the following round.

Cologne were a star-studded outfit containing several West German international players, but they could not break down Liverpool's strong, towering defence in the first leg in Germany.

The return leg at a snowbound Anfield did not take place on 3 March as previously planned, following a decision by the referee to postpone the match – Liverpool fans did, however, enjoy a memorable evening!

Anfield was covered in snow and gripped by ice when Cologne appeared on that freezing March evening. Cologne were keen to have the match played. They had a large contingent of supporters over for the game. They were also facing a backlog of domestic fixtures back home and were quite used to playing in snow conditions.

As the snowstorm worsened, the referee had no option but to postpone the tie. Liverpool handed out vouchers to a packed Anfield crowd informing them that the match would go ahead at a later date. The Kop took matters into their own hands. Having come to Anfield for an evening's entertainment with their friends and an escape from the trials and tribulations of everyday life, the Red-necks were not for returning home so early. A mass snowball fight ensued with 'opposing' teams from the Kop and Anfield Road ends of Anfield invading the pitch to 'do battle'.

Shankly stood in the stand and surveyed the scene. Thousands of men and boys engaged in a snow fight, rolling around on the snow-covered pitch, laughing, joking and hugging each other. They were at Anfield, their own back garden! The police were told to leave the fans to it. In any case, the Kop gates had frozen and they couldn't get out. The laughter continued until the fans slowly made their way home – it had been another great night out at Anfield.

The match was reconvened two weeks later, resulting in another 0–0 draw. Following a further draw, this time 2–2 in neutral Rotterdam, the European Cup-tie was decided on the toss of a coin. Ron Yeats called correctly; Liverpool marched on to meet Inter Milan in the semi-final.

This was a great achievement. Hibernian and Manchester United were the only two British clubs to have come this far in the European Cup.

Inter Milan were known to Liverpool, having eliminated Everton in the previous year's European competition. They would indeed be formidable opposition with their galaxy of Italian internationals managed by top tactician and coach Helena Merrera.

Before this European tie, however, Liverpool were to be engaged in FA Cup final duty at Wembley. As Liverpool's league fortunes had sagged, FA Cup glory had become a real prospect during the '64–'65 season. The Kop were beside themselves as the Reds disposed of West Brom, Stockport County, Bolton and Leicester before facing Tommy Docherty's fancied young Chelsea outfit in the FA Cup semifinal at Villa Park. Goals from Peter Thompson and a Willie Stevenson penalty sent the Red Army on their way to Wembley.

The city was abuzz with talk about football. Inter Milan in the European Cup final but, firstly, an FA Cup final against Don Revie's Leeds United. So what if Liverpool didn't win the league? There were other fish for the Scouse legions to fry.

The scramble to secure FA Cup final tickets was on. Shankly's office was besieged by fans requesting access to the big match at Wembley. It seemed all Merseyside was intent on making the trek to London to witness Liverpool lifting the FA trophy. Ness and her husband took the trouble to reply to every written request for a ticket.

It was said that left to Shankly, every Liverpool fan would have been given a voucher for the match – he was outraged on hearing London touts were selling the sought-after tickets at grossly inflated prices. Wembley was covered in a sea of red as Liverpool and Leeds United contested the 1965 FA Cup final. Liverpudlians were all the more determined to see their heroes lift the trophy on seeing former Everton star Bobby Collins in the Leeds line-up.

Just before kick-off, Shankly had a run-in with Inter Milan's Signor Sorti, who had come to 'spy' on their European Cup opponents.

'Are your team used to hearing a lot of noise?' asked Shankly of Sorti.

Sorti replied that the Italians themselves had a vociferous support and that they had experienced 'the Liverpool noise on our visit to Goodison Park'.

'That's nothing,' replied Shankly. 'You haven't heard noise until you've heard our supporters!'

Even on Cup final day at Wembley, Shankly was preparing for the European tie, winning a psychological battle by placing the seed of fear into the mind of the Milan 'spy'.

The Cup final ended in a 0–0 draw after 90 minutes. As extra time was about to commence, it was revealed that Gerry Byrne had broken his collar bone. He was strapped up and sent out for the extra 15 minutes which would decide the Cup's destiny. Hunt opened the scoring for Liverpool, but a Billy Bremner equaliser hushed the Liverpool fans until, with a replay looming, Ian St John headed in the winner which was to take the FA Cup to Anfield for the first time in the club's 73-year history.

Wembley exploded into noise as the Scouse legions celebrated. Each player's name was chanted until, in unison, the roar of 'Shankly – Shankly – Shankly' reverberated around the domes of the Empire Stadium.

Following the trophy presentation, Shankly, bedecked in a supporter's scarf, went over to salute the terracings packed with Liverpool fans. He knew just how much this Cup win meant to the people. As the fans at Wembley sang 'Ee-aye-addio – we've won the Cup', tens of thousands back home on Merseyside celebrated in typical fashion. The eyes of Britain were on the great city as it danced and sang its way through the day. It was VE-day all over again as all Merseyside awaited the return of their heroes.

The following day, Lime Street Station was packed as over 50,000 people turned out to welcome the arrival of Liverpool and the FA Cup. The streets of the city were brought to a standstill as over quarter of a million people made their way to Liverpool Town Hall to acclaim their heroes.

Liverpool reverberated to the chants of 'Liv-er-pool! Liv-er-pool!' as an open-top bus conveyed Shankly and his boys with the FA Cup down Lime Street towards the city centre. An emotional Shankly is said to have shed tears throughout the journey, which ended at Liverpool Town Hall where it was reported that almost the entire population of Liverpool had gathered to catch a glimpse of the FA Cup.

Three days after the victorious return from Wembley, Liverpool were on European Cup semi-final duty against Inter Milan. Half of the city was still celebrating the FA Cup success, the other half desperately scrambling to get tickets for the big match.

From early morning the streets in Liverpool's Anfield area were so crammed that the police instructed Liverpool FC to open the gates in the afternoon to let the gathering crowd into the stadium. Anfield stadium was packed around tea-time as tens of thousands of workers made their way straight to the match. Factories which normally operated a late shift closed down as workers left their tools, making their way to the ground to cheer the Reds on in their quest for European glory.

Shankly quickly seized upon the advantage that the packed, noisy stadium would provide. Asking the Italians to take to the field, he held his own squad behind. The reception Milan received was unnerving and they remembered Shankly's warning that they would encounter supporters the likes of whom they had never seen before.

Racing to the Kop end for the pre-match kick-about, they were so frightened by the roaring, swaying masses behind the goal that they immediately turned on their heels and sprinted towards the opposite Anfield Road goal. The 'welcome' there proved to be just as hostile. A few minutes later the second psychological battle was won as Liverpool took to the field amidst an explosion of sound which, it is said, could be heard several miles away from Anfield.

There was more to come in the Shankly scheme to 'frighten the opposition to death'.

Milne and Byrne, the injured FA Cup heroes, appeared on the pitch carrying the trophy. As the two 'crocks' hobbled around the pitch perimeter holding the glittering prize up for all to see, the Anfield crowd went into hysterics. For a few minutes Inter Milan and the European Cup were forgotten as tears were shed and the 55,000 crowd chanted 'Ee-aye-addio, we've got the Cup'.

The Italians were visibly shaken by this mass demonstration of euphoria. Even their own excitable Latin temperaments were nothing compared to the fervour and fanaticism which they had just witnessed.

Hunt sent the Anfield throng into seventh heaven as he opened the scoring in the first few minutes. The Italians were reeling with shock but composed themselves somewhat to square through a goal by Mazzola. Goals by Callaghan and St John, however, gave Liverpool victory in the first-leg tie and a comfortable two-goal advantage to take to Milan.

A tragic incident, though, shook a city in celebration the following day as the news broke that Jimmy McInnes, Liverpool's club secretary for the past ten years, was found hanged at one of the Kemlyn Road turnstiles. McInnes's suicide was attributed to the heavy workload he incurred during this period of Liverpool's fantastic success.

Liverpool's European joy was short-lived as, two weeks later, in the San Siro stadium, Milan scored the three goals required to take them to the European Cup final.

Milan had turned the tables on Liverpool, whipping their 90,000 crowd into hysteria before the start of a game which was shrouded in controversy: firstly, the Italians scored directly from an indirect free kick, then Peiro kicked the ball from goalkeeper Tommy Lawrence's hands to score a second. Milan's cynical tackling and some extremely dubious refereeing decisions unsettled Liverpool who conceded a third goal as tempers frayed and arguments raged over the referee's 'neutrality'.

Shankly was incensed. His boys had been robbed but, lifting their spirits in his inimitable way, Shankly told the boys on their return home: 'Okay, boys, we've lost, but see what we've done to Milan, the unofficial champions of the world. All these people are overjoyed because they've beaten Liverpool – that's the standard you have raised yourselves to!'

He was right. Milan were a millionaires club whose team included the great Sandro Mazzola, Fachetti, Jair and the Spanish international Peiro. Their coach, Herrera, was hailed as the greatest tactician in the European game.

Liverpool, and Shankly, had learned lessons; they had a while to go yet before European Cup success would come Anfield's way. They were, however, on the right road. Not bad for an outfit who less than four years earlier had been struggling to gain promotion from the Second Division.

Shankly was fast becoming a legend in Liverpool. His rapport with the ordinary supporter was uncanny.

During the past five years he had bonded both club and supporter; Liverpool FC was a family. Shankly would move heaven and earth to assist with any problem large or small when asked by a fan, and when match tickets came into his possession, he would pass them around the supporters.

Tommy Docherty recalled an incident when, before a Chelsea versus Liverpool league game at Stamford Bridge, Shankly, aware that a train-load of ticketless Liverpool fans had made the journey to London, asked Chelsea for 500 tickets and promised Chelsea that they would have a similar free allocation when they came to Anfield.

Clutching the tickets, Shankly made his way amongst the Liverpudlians standing outside Stamford Bridge with their 'trannies' waiting to listen to the match broadcast.

'There you go, son. Here you are, boys. That's for you, son.' The hero distributed the tickets to an ecstatic crowd.

Some saw this behaviour as eccentric but to Shankly and the Scousers, nothing could have been more natural.

17

Liverpool is on the Map

By the mid-'60s, the city of Liverpool had established itself as contender for the title of 'Finest City in the Empire'.

Britain's Prime Minister, Harold Wilson, came from the Wirral and represented the Huyton constituency. The 'Liverpool sound' was top of the pops on radio, jukeboxes and record players in every corner of the universe.

The Beatles, Gerry and the Pacemakers, Billy J. Kramer and The Dakotas had people of every nation swinging to the 'Mersey beat'. Liverpool and Everton had both been League champions whilst the Red Army's glorious cup runs on the domestic and European scenes had captured the imagination of soccer fans far beyond the banks of the Mersey.

The Liver Bird had become as famous an English landmark as London's Big Ben; the Scouse accent once dismissed as 'guttural' was the accent everyone wanted to hear; the Beatles were attracting more foreign revenue as a tourist attraction than the royal family. Merseyside knew that this new feel-good factor was attributable to a great extent to the efforts of the manager at Anfield. At this time, Shankly's fixation with American gangsterism was becoming legendary. His Jimmy Cagney swagger, the cocked trilby hat and the knee-length raincoat caused great amusement among

Liverpudlians. Players would be shown pictures of his heroes.

Ron Yeats recalled: 'He would show you pictures of Eliot Ness, Bugsy Moran or Cagney saying, "You think you're a hard man, when these guys do something wrong they get shot – these are hard men!"'

Friday evenings were spent at home with Ness watching Shankly's hero Eliot Ness in 'The Untouchables' series, but when the team left for a Friday overnight stay in Liverpool FC's hotel before an away match, the coach would conveniently arrive at the hotel in perfect time for the manager to settle in his room for another episode featuring Ness and his agents.

Shankly and Liverpool swaggered into the 1965–66 league season. Aberdeen's goalkeeper John 'Tubby' Ogston had been signed as a cover keeper for £10,000. By Christmas, Liverpool were top of the league and, although their FA Cup run had been halted by Tommy Docherty's young Chelsea in the third round, there was the prospect of glory in the European Cup Winners Cup which Liverpool had entered by virtue of the previous season's FA Cup win.

Juventus of Italy were accounted for by a 2–1 aggregate over two legs. Standard Liege of Belgium and Hungary's Honved were also disposed of before Liverpool were drawn against Glasgow Celtic in the competition's semi-final.

Before the Celtic tie, however, Shankly had sent the Liverpool fans wild with delight over a 5–0 drubbing of arch-rivals Everton. Prior to this local derby, Shankly and Paisley had visited Everton's training ground at Bellefield to watch Harry Catterick put his Blues through their paces.

Everton were a fine side, but with a view to boosting the psychology of his own men, as always, he informed them: 'We've just been over to see Everton train. They'll be knackered by Saturday the way Catterick has them running around.'

All the players knew Paisley was a gambling man and were impressed when Shankly turned to him saying: 'Get the best odds you can for us on a Liverpool victory against Everton on Saturday.'

On the match day, Shankly greeted the visiting Everton team then burst into Liverpool's dressing-room yelling: 'Boys, they can hardly walk – they look shattered!'

Shankly's boys responded to this coaching by tearing into Everton from the kick-off, soaring to a memorable 5–0 victory.

Liverpool travelled to Glasgow for the Cup-Winners Cup semi-final against a Celtic side managed by Shankly's old friend Jock Stein. Knowing that a two- or three-goal cushion would be required if they were to survive at Anfield, Celtic piled on the pressure but could only manage one strike past a solid Liverpool defence.

Anfield was packed to overflowing as Celtic's fanatical support converged upon Liverpool for the semi-final second leg, which the Reds won by two goals scored by Smith and Strong.

Shortly after this match, Liverpool were again crowned First Division champions and made ready for the Cup-Winners final to be held at Hampden Park, Glasgow, against Borussia Dortmund of Germany.

A rain-lashed Hampden Park was understandably half empty as 41,000 fans – mostly from Merseyside – huddled together to watch the 1965–66 European Cup-Winners Cup final. At the end of 90 minutes the score stood at one each.

The heavens opened up and poured down on Hampden Park as Liverpool and Dortmund slipped and slithered to the end of extra time which saw the Germans score a second and Cup-winning goal.

European success had yet again eluded Shankly and his Red Army, who nevertheless had plenty to cheer about as the league championship had been secured.

Liverpudlians would also celebrate, with the rest of the country, England's momentous 1966 World Cup victory over West Germany, not least because Liverpool and Everton had supplied the English World Cup squad with Peter Thompson, Gordon Milne, Roger Hunt, Ian Callaghan, Alan Ball and Ray Wilson. Of these, Hunt, Ball and Wilson participated in the World Cup final.

The city of Liverpool was, rightly, proud of their contribution to England's World Cup glory. Shankly, however, was not over-impressed by the competition which he said had thrown up negative, defensive teams. 'Apart from Portugal, Hungary and Brazil, they were all defensive. England peaked and played like a good English club side, that's why they beat West Germany.'

Prior to the start of the '66–'67 league season, Liverpool and Everton paraded the World Cup around Goodison Park in the FA Charity Shield final, but as Merseyside gave tumultuous acclaim to their World Cup heroes, Shankly began to ponder the future.

His Anfield stars were beginning to age and were, ironically, victims of their own success. His squad were involved not only in league and cup duty on the domestic front, but a majority were called upon for international duties too, and the European campaign had taken its toll. Shankly had grown with his boys; he loved them all as a father would love his sons. Liverpool's greatness stemmed from the great team spirit, the 'family' environment he had built around Anfield. Shankly, his boys and the fans had come through a lot together in the past six years, but a watershed was being reached. Did he carry on with these men out of sentiment or loyalty, or would a new squad, fit to win more success, require to be assembled? He remembered Arsenal during the war. Yet how do you tell Tommy Smith and the boys, who had brought so much joy to the city of Liverpool, that they were nearing the end?

Shankly had to face facts. Like all other teams, Liverpool had reached a period where transformation would have to take place. Team restructuring and building for the future would have to be embarked upon if Liverpool were to move out of the '60s and into the '70s. The European Cup would have to adorn the Anfield trophy cabinet as a measure of real success for the club.

18

The Long and Winding Road

Many English football fans, including a few Liverpudlians, look back on the period between 1966 and 1973 as 'the seven years Liverpool won nothing'.

While, statistically, this may be correct, Liverpool were still the team to beat during these seasons in which Shankly was 'rebuilding for the '70s'.

During season 1971–72 Liverpool had been extremely powerful in reaching the FA Cup final and had reached the semi-final of the European Cup-Winners Cup.

The crowds still packed into Anfield as, season by season, Shankly added to the club's playing strengths. A major signing in 1967 had been the appointment of former Northern Ireland manager Geoff Twentyman as Liverpool's chief scout. Rather than plunge into a transfer market where players were exchanging clubs for £100,000-plus fees, Shankly reverted to 'building from within'.

His reserve teams would produce the Anfield stars of the future. Liverpool would identify the best young talent, buy them at a pinch and groom them in the Liverpool way.

Big names could cause problems in the changing-room. There must surely be plenty of lads from Lancashire, Cheshire, Wirral and Wales who could be brought into the

Liverpool family and become Liverpool men – fit to wear the red jersey.

Players' wages had spiralled during the '60s. Liverpool were not renowned for paying their players huge salaries – Shankly believed that footballers should not become middle class by earning more than their supporters– big money transfer men, on the other hand, would expect big wages. No one at Liverpool was paid more than his team-mates, which was a pay structure few outside Anfield would have favoured. That was the difference. Players coming to Anfield would arrive desperate to play for the club, not for financial gain. Those who were identified as Liverpool 'material' would be watched week after week before they were eventually signed.

Shankly's welcome to new faces would be: 'Son, when you come here we'll be watching your every move. Every second of the day you'll be under the eye of me and my staff.'

This was the Anfield way. Liverpool were run on strict discipline such that every meal players ate, for example, was pre-planned. Football to Shankly was 'a kind of socialism', requiring his players to give 100 per cent commitment to the club: his Red Army was indeed a disciplined unit.

Another great Shankly story involves both diet and commitment. A player, who shall remain nameless, was assessed by Shankly as being in need of 'feeding up'. The youngster was fed on a diet of thick steaks and eggs for several months until one day he approached Shankly asking for a Saturday off to get married.

'Married,' retorted Shankly. 'You can't get married now, son. It's the middle of the season. I got married in the close-season .'

'But, Boss,' pleaded the lad, 'I have to get married, she's pregnant.'

On hearing this, Shankly turned to Bob Paisley yelling: 'For Christ sake, stop the steaks! We've bred a bloody sex monster!'

With the emphasis on grooming young talent, Joe Fagan took firm control of Liverpool's reserves, while during the period 1966 to 1973 some significant signings were made.

During 1966, Emlyn Hughes arrived from Blackpool; in 1967 Tony Hateley was brought in from Chelsea; and in 1968 Ray Clemence and Alec Lindsay entered Anfield. Larry Lloyd joined Liverpool in 1969, and between 1970–73, Steve Heighway, John Toshack, Kevin Keegan, Trevor Storton, Peter Cormack and Alan Waddle were drafted in to join youngsters such as Phil Boersma, Doug Livermore and Brian Hall who were steadily progressing through Fagan's impressive reserve side.

These players revelled in the Anfield style of coaching. Never before had they experienced the total commitment, expertise and enthusiasm which exuded from Shankly, Paisley, Bennett and Fagan.

Brian Hall recalled an initial introduction to Shankly's wit and humour. A Preston youngster who was studying mathematics at Liverpool University, Hall had been playing in Liverpool's reserves supplementing his income by working as a bus conductor during the summer. As he went to Anfield prior to an afternoon shift on the buses, Shankly spied the young lad in his conductor's uniform. Surveying Hall's lack of height, Shankly burst out: 'Bloody hell! It looks like we've signed Jimmy Clitheroe.'

On hearing who Hall was, he added: 'Hello, son, great, aye. You're the boy from university. Tell me, laddie, do you need a university degree these days to be a bus conductor?'

Following this 'introduction' to Shankly, Hall said that on hearing he was from Preston, Shankly cornered him at every opportunity to relate countless stories of his days at Preston North End and wax lyrical on the great skills of Tom Finney.

Shankly and Paisley were systematically building their new Liverpool family, and before long, yet another phoenix would rise from the ashes in Liverpool. Shankly was extremely proud that the fans had stuck by him and the club; they had attained greatness before and would do so again. As Leeds, Arsenal and Manchester United covered themselves in glory, Liverpool were diligently working to shape, build and prepare themselves for the '70s. Anfield stadium, too, was part of this transitionary period.

The fans' loyalty was being repaid through the first phases of reconstruction which would provide a stadium of which the city would be proud. At Melwood too, facilities were being transformed.

Shankly had initially 'taken the place by the scruff of the neck' and provided great entertainment for the faithful on Saturdays and at evening weekday matches. The man himself was an entertaining figure – the Jimmy Cagney look-alike, who had a joke for every occasion, had endeared himself to all Liverpool. They were certainly going to stand by him during the barren years because they had faith in the man's ability to restore former glories. That's what he had told them he would do, after all. He was accorded the honour given to few – an adopted Scouser.

Although the trophy room was bare during this period, Shankly's new team was beginning to emerge. Mighty Arsenal had become League champions in 1970–71, but when the new Red Army of Clemence, Hall, Hughes, Evans, Thompson, Toshack and Heighway defeated the arch-enemy Everton in the FA Cup semi-final at Old Trafford, Liverpool's spark was rekindled. In the Wembley final, Liverpool held the Gunners to a one each draw at the end of 90 minutes before going down 2–1 in extra time.

All Liverpool eagerly awaited the start of the '72–'73 season. The Reds had shown during the period 1970 to 1972 that they were on the way back. A fine team had been built, a team fit to bring success in the '70s. The added propositions of classy ex-Hibernian and Notts Forest star Peter Cormack and the 19-year-old Kevin Keegan had the Kop eager to get on with it.

Brian Hall says that a major component in the success that was to follow was 'mutual respect, total respect'. 'We respected Shankly, he respected us. We all respected the fans who returned that respect. We had become a total team.'

Emlyn Hughes added that the team was playing 'total football; everyone in the side was a winner and knew how to play'.

This concept of 'total football' was to be accredited to the

Holland team of the 1974 World Cup but was in fact a feature of Shanklyism for many years before. Shankly's team as it entered the '70s was also intelligent in that they knew what he was about and knew the type of football he wanted them to play.

Shankly himself said: 'Every player in my team has to play for the team, not himself. Here, we do things collectively. We have specialist players in specialist positions. We don't complicate them so that each player has a simple job to do.'

Players were encouraged to consider themselves as a family, 'brothers' who could talk freely with each other and help each other.

One player who was over-critical of one of his struggling team-mates was asked by Shankly: 'Laddie, what would you do if your neighbour's house was on fire? Get out there, son, and help him!'

With this camaraderie and enormous confidence in their abilities, Liverpool would send the Kop once again into raptures as they stormed to the 1972–73 championship title. This was the team Shankly had dreamed of producing.

Other honours would come Liverpool and Shankly's way over the next two years. That European glory, which had proved so elusive in the past, would be his before he was to leave Anfield.

19

Manager of the Year

As season 1972–73 commenced, Liverpool fans flooding into the restored Anfield stadium could have no idea of what the next two years would bring. Tom Saunders had been brought into the Liverpool engine-house of the boot room and Shankly's coaching team were ready to lead their red storm-troops into league and European success with Liverpool qualifying to enter the UEFA Cup.

Shankly was very close to his playing staff. He knew what made them tick. Brian Hall said: 'He was a father figure who would listen to you, sort out any individual problems a player had and would take away any pressure, allowing you to concentrate fully on your game.'

Shankly's humour was an important factor in settling people. When John Toshack arrived with his wife at Lime Street Station to sign for Liverpool, Shankly, on meeting the couple, noticed Tosh's wife was wearing a blue coat.

'You'd better get rid of that, lassie,' he said. 'We're red here.'

Players thrived in an atmosphere where the manager was always available. They had great respect for a gaffer who would be first on the scene at Anfield, attending to business from 8 a.m., and who would be last to leave the stadium in the evening when the day's work was done. Shankly could lose his temper, but he was quick to calm down again, never parting with a player on bad terms. The total respect Shankly had for his players showed itself in his dealings with the press. Whilst he would criticise his team or individuals for poor performances within the confines of Anfield stadium, he would never air these criticisms in public.

The city of Liverpool needed the lift which the 1972–73 season was to provide. The blight of unemployment was still around as Britain moved towards entry into what was then the Common Market. Gone was the Mersey beat of the '60s: Cammell Laird's shipyard in Birkenhead was in rapid decline; Merseyside, like most industrial areas of Britain, was moving towards the dark days of industrial action as workers took to the streets in protest at rising unemployment and attacks on wages and conditions by Government and employers; shipping and dock work had moved to ports on the eastern seaboard.

Liverpool FC had to rise once more to the occasion, and they did. Capacity crowds of 50,000 crammed into Anfield each Saturday match day, welcoming the brief respite from the industrial unrest which surrounded their working lives. If job insecurity was causing stress in their daily existence, at least they were relaxed enough at Anfield to indulge in a day's entertainment, an escape from the harsh realities of life. Shankly knew only too well how hard things were for these people. He would constantly remind his players of their duty, their obligation to give 100 per cent in providing entertainment and excitement for the Anfield faithful who had come along at a time of great financial insecurity to hand over their cash at the turnstiles. Liverpool did not let the people down. During a season in which they lost only a handful of games, Shankly's boys clinched the league title in front of a packed Anfield, drawing their final match with Leicester City.

Pandemonium ensued as Shankly and the team did a lap of honour around the ground. Wearing a red shirt and matching red tie for the occasion, Shankly walked over to the Kop punching the air. Anfield's stands shook as the chant of

'Shankly! – Shankly! – Shankly!' screamed from the throats of the jubilant Red-necks.

As fans invaded the pitch, mobbing their heroes, a policeman kicked aside a scarf which had been thrown onto the pitch by an ecstatic Kop-ite. On seeing this, Shankly pushed the young officer aside, saying: 'Don't be doing that. That's someone's life.'

There can be no doubt that the signing of Kevin Keegan was a Shankly masterstroke. The pairing of Keegan and Toshack in Liverpool's forward line devastated opposition defences during the race for the '72–'73 league title and contributed immensely to the Red march to European success that season.

Keegan was a likeable young man who, like Shankly, came from mining stock. His father and grandfather had both worked in the mines as had Shankly. This created a bond between the two which Keegan cherishes to this day. 'He made me welcome at Anfield from the first day; I respected the man dearly.'

Keegan, like others before him, revelled in the atmosphere at Anfield. Shankly 'was interested in his players as people'. There's no doubt that Shankly's continual public insistence that Keegan was a tremendous player with natural ability and inner strength boosted the player's confidence immensely. Shankly had learned from his European experiences of the '60s and passed this knowledge on to his '70s team. Liverpool played a 'European' game against the continentals, slowing the game down in away legs, rarely giving the ball away, while in home legs, they played the short passing game then attacked at a ferocious pace.

Eintracht Frankfurt, AEK Athens, Dynamo Berlin and Dynamo Dresden were disposed of before UEFA Cup-holders Tottenham were defeated in the semi-final. Liverpool were only a two-leg UEFA Cup final away from Shankly's dream of European glory. The whole of Liverpool prayed for victory. Not only for the team and the city, but for Shankly. They knew how much it would mean to him to parade a piece of European silverware through the streets of his adopted city.

Liverpool's Cup final opponents were the impressive Borussia Moenchengladbach, a tremendous side comprising West German internationalists who had recently trumped England 3–1 at Wembley. Players like Bertie Vogts, Ove Simmonsen, Gunter Netzer and Danner were household names throughout Europe. Would Shankly's boys be a match for such talent or would it once more be a case of a bridge too far? Liverpool answered the sceptics! The first-leg match at Anfield was abandoned after half an hour (due to torrential rain), and scheduled to be played the following day. Having had a glimpse of the Germans during the abandoned match, Shankly altered his side. Originally, Shankly, on hearing reports that Borrusia could cope easily with a towering forward like Toshack, had dropped the Welsh centre. Outraged at the possibility of missing out on a European medal, Toshack had stormed out of Anfield demanding a transfer. As he arrived at his Formby home, Toshack received a telephone call from Shankly.

'Hello, son, not in bed yet? Well, you'd better turn in – there's a very good chance you'll be playing tomorrow!'

Next day, the Toshack–Keegan pairing stunned Borussia who lost 3–0 with two goals scored by Keegan and one from Larry Lloyd. Toshack's aerial menace in the penalty box could not be contained by the German defence who were up against a player out to prove to his boss that he was worthy of a European final medal!

In the return match, Borussia threw everything but the kitchen sink at Liverpool. The damage, though, had been done at Anfield. Although the Germans scored two goals, Liverpool's stout defence and midfield held out until full-time.

This was the moment Shankly had been waiting for. He brought a European trophy back to Liverpool. His new Red Army, a team mostly in their early twenties, had at last scaled the heights in Europe. The Reds had beaten the continentals at their own game: playing from the back, it was all about possession football with a slow build-up before releasing the ball to Keegan or Toshack. It was a devastating formula that got results.

Shankly drummed into his players that they were so good, opponents couldn't take the ball from them – if they didn't give it away the result would be inevitable. Even Liverpool were taken aback at the thousands who converged upon Speke Airport as the victorious Reds returned home at 1 a.m. the following morning with the UEFA Cup. Once more the city was in party mood. There was certainly a lot to celebrate: Liverpool were League champions and UEFA Cup winners, and now English football had honoured Shankly by presenting him with the Manager of the Year trophy. The season could not end, however, without a typical Shankly story.

Pleased with their players' efforts during the season, Liverpool's directors decided to give them a wage rise. Brian Hall recalled:

'We all had to go in and see the boss individually and tell him just how much of a rise we thought we were worth. Well, we thought, if we ask for £40 he'll bump us down to £30; if we ask for £80 he'll knock it down to £50. We all decided to ask for £80 per week. So I went in.

"Hello, son," said Shankly. "What do you think you're worth?"

'"I think a rise of £80 a week, Boss," I said.

'"Fine, son – send the next one in."

'We were furious,' said Hall. 'It transpired that the club were prepared to offer each of us a £100 rise. Shankly had us trembling and settling for £80.'

20

Leaving Liverpool

Season 1973–74 was Shankly's last at Anfield. Although his departure was to be tinged with sadness and regret, the abdication would be preceded by a memorable bow out at Wembley. The European Cup which Shankly had striven to bring to Anfield would not arrive in time since, following a first-leg aggregate victory over Jeunesse Esche of Luxembourg, Liverpool were eliminated from that competition by Red Star Belgrade.

Shankly was never to join the ranks of his contemporaries Jock Stein and Matt Busby in bringing the prestigious European trophy to Britain. He had, however, laid the foundations for Bob Paisley to achieve this at a later date.

Despite a strong challenge in defence of their league championship title during season '73–'74, Liverpool ended that campaign second to an impressive Leeds United, finishing five points behind Don Revie's young Yorkshire team. Shankly would, however, present the Kop with a leaving present just before his departure. Following FA Cup wins over Doncaster, Carlisle, Ipswich, Bristol City and Leicester, Liverpool were paired with Newcastle United in the Wembley final.

This was to become an extremely emotional event for

Shankly and the massive Liverpool contingent who made the pilgrimage to London.

Newcastle had been quietly tipped to give Liverpool a game of it in the FA Cup final. Their captain, Scottish internationalist Bobby Moncur, marshalled a strong United defence which was not in the habit of giving away goals easily.

United's free-scoring centre forward, England internationalist Malcolm Macdonald, was the darling of the Geordies. Macdonald angered Shankly when the United striker took it upon himself to brag to the national press that Newcastle would thrash Liverpool at Wembley. He got his answer when two goals from Keegan and another from Steve Heighway, in a final completely dominated by Liverpool, sent the red hordes once more into ecstasy.

The scenes which followed this victory have not been seen in the Empire Stadium Wembley before or since. Those who witnessed the 1973–74 Cup final, whether at Wembley or on TV, agree that Liverpool's display on the day was masterful. Time and again the eyes of the nation focused on the figure of a rugged Scot sitting on the Liverpool bench nodding to his players as they got a move right, gesticulating to them if they got it wrong. The Liverpool manager constantly barked instructions at his team and exhorted his players to build up pressure and maintain that pressure on a Newcastle side who had no answer to Liverpool's fitness.

Shankly had the last laugh on Macdonald, saying: 'He won that one for us. He liked the sound of his own voice. He spent the whole week talking about what he was going to do to us. He talked, we won!'

Following the trophy presentation, Shankly stepped onto the Wembley turf, again adorned in a Liverpool supporter's scarf. Arms outstretched, fist clenched, he walked over to the crowds of Liverpool fans to take what was to be his final bow. Several fans invaded the pitch to shake his hand, pat his back – a few knelt and kissed the feet of their hero. Again, London reverberated to the after-match chants of 'Shankly! – Shankly! – Shankly!' as Scousers celebrated the trophy win in style.

The civic reception which followed had Liverpudlians out

in their tens of thousands cheering the open-top bus carrying Shankly, his boys and the FA Cup through the packed streets to a heroes' welcome at St George's Hall.

Recalling that journey, Brian Hall said: 'As we moved through the streets waving to the crowds, Shanks said to me, "Son, you've been to university, you're a bright lad. Tell me, what's the name of that wee Chinaman with the wee book who has all the people following him?"

'I replied, "Why, it's Chairman Mao, Boss", wondering what on earth he was on about.

'Shankly replied: "Aye, son, that's him, Chairman Mao. That's the fellow."'

A little while later whilst standing on the balcony at St George's Hall in the company of civic dignitaries and the players, Shankly was waving to the crowds who were cheering and singing.

Hall remembers: 'The noise was deafening. Suddenly Shanks lifted his arms in the air, gesticulating to the crowd that he wanted silence. Immediately you could have heard a pin drop as tens of thousands obeyed his command. Then the speech.'

Shankly announced: 'Chairman Mao has never seen a greater show of Red strength than today.'

Hall smiled and thought to himself, 'Why you clever old so-and-so.'

As the strains of 'You'll Never Walk Alone' sounded out in Liverpool that evening, Scousers had no idea that this would be the last occasion on which their great idol would address them.

Shankly did, however, allow himself one parting shot, when on receiving an OBE, awarded to him for his services to football, he typically announced that the honour was not for him – 'it was for the people of Liverpool and Liverpool FC'.

Aye! Glenbuck teaching. A victory for one was a victory for all.

British football at this time was dominated by three Scots, men of similar backgrounds who had been born within a few miles of each other. The names of Shankly, Busby and Stein were known and respected throughout Britain and Europe as master tacticians and first-class coaches. All three had an almost identical philosophy on how football should be played and became legends in their own lifetimes.

Busby went on to receive a knighthood for his contribution to the great game but it still rankles with Liverpool fans that Shankly only received an OBE.

As the media gathered at Anfield on 12 July 1974 to witness the public showing of new signing Ray Kennedy from Arsenal, they had no idea of the headline which was to follow chairman John Smith's introduction of the player.

Even the most experienced of journalists were shaken as Smith announced: 'It is with great regret that, as chairman of the board, I have to inform you that Mr Shankly has intimated to us that he wishes to retire from league football.'

Silence followed.

Shankly, who didn't look his usual jaunty self, then informed the press corps: 'This is not a decision that was taken quickly. It has been on my mind over the last twelve months and I feel it is time I took a rest from the game I've served for 43 years. My wife and I both felt we wanted to have a rest and charge up my batteries again.'

Shankly added that the decision to retire had been the hardest of his life. 'It was like walking to the electric chair. I was going to be burned up, frizzled up.'

He assured the fans that he and Ness would continue to live in their adopted city and, visibly shaken, looking for the first time like a man in his sixties, concluded: 'When a new man comes in, I will be out. It will be a complete break but I'll still come to watch Liverpool and, when I do, I'll want them to win. I'll probably go into the Kop.'

The reaction which greeted the news was one of stunned shock. Merseyside could not believe that Shankly was going. Then – 'Nah, it's only one of Bill's tantrums. He's threatened to go before.'

'Old Bill retiring? No way. He'll be back.'

'He just needs a bit of a holiday.'

The people refused to accept that Shankly was going. He

didn't look 61, did he? Always fit, bouncing around the city, full of confidence, bubbling with enthusiasm.

Shankly, however, was tired and Ness had been ill. They had both discussed things and came to the agreement that it was time to enjoy their remaining years quietly. Bill would spend more time with the family; they would have some quality, relaxing time together.

Although not keeping in good health herself, Ness had been more worried about her husband. 'Bill's as fit as a fiddle,' she said at the time. 'But you can be fit and still be tired. I've never really pushed him and I've always been behind any decision he made. But last year I asked him to think about retirement and it is for me that he has made this announcement.'

The shock which greeted the news continued. People knew that retirement was anathema to Shankly. He 'would rather have been killed in battle than captured' said old fan Tommy Solomon.

The pubs of Liverpool were strangely silent on that evening of 12 July 1974. It is said that the later demise of John Lennon was met with nowhere near the sense of loss Liverpool felt at Shankly's going.

'It was as if there had been a death in the family,' said veteran Kop-ite Tony Callaghan.

Very soon, shock turned to anger as many searched for the reasons behind Shankly's leaving. It was common knowledge that John Smith was one of a new breed of football chairmen; he was a 'hands-on' man who wanted to oversee all aspects of the club's affairs including player transfers, team matters, public relations and the club's financial affairs. Smith was a new moderniser; Shankly was, in today's terms, 'Old Labour'.

There was controversy over the signing of Ray Kennedy from Arsenal. Shankly's 'contract' with Liverpool which gave him free rein over the buying and selling of players stopped when John Smith took the helm in the boardroom. Liverpool had returned to the policy where directors vetted all players considered for transfer to Anfield.

Power which had previously been devolved to Shankly was taken back. He no longer had full say in wage negotiations or public relations, and media releases would be conducted by a new breed of 'professionals'. Shankly had never been one to sit through boardroom meetings discussing club affairs. He had little time for such 'distractions'. Shankly was a manager. He managed the club in all matters from coaching, team selection and transfers to interaction with the public and media. Under three previous chairmen – T.V. Williams, Sydney Reakes and Eric Roberts – he had been given full scope to develop his own style, install his regime, build his empire. Eric Sawyer had recognised Shankly's potential for success and encouraged and supported his style.

Smith could not have taken Shankly on during the '60s, but the great manager was older now, weary from a lifetime's work. Rather than defend his corner, fight yet another boardroom battle, he had to walk away. Bill was seen as 'old-time'. In order to get results he had to work long hours, involve himself in every issue, keep his finger fully on the pulse. Now, directors expected younger managers to be more objective and answer directly to the new breed of all-powerful chairmen. Shankly saw this as a facet of class war. Having wrested power from the 'ruling class' at Anfield, it was now being taken back. He had been usurped.

To be fair to Smith, although he felt it was time for Shankly to go as manager, he was offered a position. A new post of general manager would be created allowing Shankly to work towards eventual retirement, working whatever hours he wished on a quite generous salary. After all, Matt Busby had assumed this new role at Manchester United. Smith pleaded with Shankly to remain at Anfield, relaxing into eventual retiral: he knew the effect the great man's going would have on fans' morale.

Shankly was adamant. He had said he wanted a rest from football for a while, and perhaps he wanted Liverpool to say, 'Okay, Bill, take some time out. Rest up, then come back in a year or two.' This was never an option. He felt that his 'power base' had been eroded to such an extent that the manager at Liverpool would become a 'puppet' in the boardroom. Football politics had changed. Bill was part of an ancient regime that was being replaced by the new hands-on directors looking to develop the football business in other directions.

Really, there was no place for Shankly's charisma. He had done the job, taken the place by the scruff of the neck and shaken it into the twentieth century. Others would take it into the twenty-first.

Shankly was hurt. He had never worked at Anfield 'for the wages'. Financial reward or the OBE were never motivating forces. He had given body and soul to Liverpool FC but his ego had been sorely dented by the new people who had invaded his territory. Unlike his old friend Jock Stein at Celtic Park, Shankly was never offered a directorship at Anfield. Perhaps in quoting Mao he had given a clue. Would the title of honorary chairman suffice? His leaving Liverpool was to be shrouded in bitterness.

One regret Shankly did have of his time at Anfield was that he never asked for, nor demanded, a huge salary. He had never invested in the future nor taken opportunities to earn extra wages through sideline jobs. He had never really thought about nor prepared for the financial aspects of retirement. He and Ness had always lived in the same modest home in Bellefield Avenue.

He would have to find other sources of income for the remaining years until his official pensionable age of 65!

21

You'll Never Walk Alone

Friction between Shankly and Liverpool continued after his leaving. Shankly just couldn't let go. Leading Liverpool sides out in the FA Charity Shield match at Wembley and a testimonial game for Billy McNeill a few days later at Celtic Park were not occasions used by the man to say farewell to the fans. They were statements that he was not down and out. Sadly, perhaps, Shankly anticipated that the fans would apply tremendous pressure on Liverpool's board. He may have expected the 'Shankly Must Stay' banners, boycotts of Liverpool games or some other gestures of 'solidarity' which would rescue the situation. As he slipped into retirement, problems arose which hurt Shankly deeply and caused pain among those who loved him so dearly.

Liverpool had looked at two or three prospective managers before agreeing that Bob Paisley was to be Shankly's successor. Shankly himself had recommended Paisley to the board. Paisley, in turn, paid homage to his predecessor by commenting that the work had already been done, and that he was 'just taking over Bill's team'.

'Taking over', however, was not going to be that easy! Shankly was like a lioness whose cubs were being threatened. Liverpool had given him permission to work out at Melwood training ground, and it was here that Banquo's ghost caused problems by constantly chatting to players and involving himself in their training activities. This wasn't fair to Paisley who needed to make his own mark as manager and stamp his authority on players. Consequently, Liverpool politely asked Shankly to carry out his exercises in the afternoons when business with the players at Melwood had ended.

This request was, and is, seen by most Liverpudlians as insensitive on Liverpool's part. Everyone knew Shankly had made a mistake; he wanted to be asked back. Surely there would be a grieving time when he could be allowed to move on quietly.

Stories that he was not welcome in the Liverpool directors' box at home matches or that he had to ask for a match ticket incensed, and still do, the Anfield faithful who, although powerless to alter things, were deeply hurt at the thought of Shankly being mistreated by the club.

Shankly fuelled these feelings by intimating he'd rather stand on the Kop with his friends, the true Liverpool fans. He had made his decision and those in charge had moved on with a new manager. He would have to accept this.

The same Ayrshire stubbornness, pride, conviction and passion which had driven Shankly throughout his career were, ironically, going to cause a divide of bitterness between him and the club he loved so dearly.

Perhaps the new men, the modernisers with all the intellect and sophistication which that breed purported to possess, could have handled Shankly's retiral with more thought, more humility and greater dignity.

Fan Ray O'Brien commented: 'A first-year social work student could have handled matters more professionally!'

The new breed of chairmen, however, wished the limelight to be on them so that they could give an impression of complete control. We can see this even today in the likes of Celtic, Rangers, Chelsea, Blackburn and Tottenham. Shankly, though, was the inextinguishable fire at Liverpool. You could almost visualise him standing on the roof of the Kop or in the centre circle at Wembley saying, in Jimmy

Cagney fashion, 'Look at me, Ma – I'm dancing,' as the city idolised him.

There was no room for managers like Shankly in the new world. Sadly, as events have shown, there is no longer any room for the type of supporter who used to pack Anfield, since corporate ticket sales, season tickets and overseas supporters club allocations have brought about the demise of the great family spirit which Shankly built. The new 'family' of Liverpool supporters who pack Anfield, who inhabit the Kop, tend to hail from outside the city – from Wales, other English counties, Scandinavia and other points on the globe. Shankly would not have been comfortable with this new wave.

His audiences were from Bootle, Dingle, Tuebrook, Wallasey, Birkenhead, Walton, Anfield, Everton Valley, Derby Road, Kirkby, Skelmersdale, Crosby and the other areas in and around his adopted city. Liverpool FC had belonged to the Scousers – that's what it was all about!

In today's economic climate, however, the sponsors, businessmen, privileged people and those who can afford to lay out several hundreds of pounds, are the ones who secure the match tickets. You won't see today's Liverpool manager handing out tickets to the faithful!

To be fair to Liverpool FC, this transition has taken place throughout the football world. The game is now big business. Players are paid £10,000 to £20,000 per week; managers command six-figure annual salaries. Shankly would never have lived in that world which was fast approaching as he departed Anfield – nor would he have wanted to!

His had been a simple, more honest world where 'football was like socialism'; unlike the 'people's game' today which belongs to the Murrays, Walkers, Haywards, Bates, Sugars and McCanns among many others.

Shankly's days had passed and with them the idea, the philosophy, that the town's football club belonged to the people – football's 'Clause Four' was scrapped from the fans' party card!

With a living to earn, Shankly busied himself in retiral. He was an experienced man, an authority on football, a character to whom people in the game would still listen. He would appear at Everton's Bellefield training ground where his advice and comments on coaching matters were welcomed and greeted with non-patronising respect by Howard Kendall and the Everton staff. Rather ironic that the arch-enemy should welcome Shankly into their coaching sessions when he was banished from Melwood!

Ron Yeats had become manager at Tranmere Rovers across the River Mersey and was quick in appointing Shankly as club consultant. Yeats said that Shankly's presence at Tranmere was an immense boost to players and fans as 'you could hear an immense buzz round the stadium when Bill appeared in the stand – if the Queen had been there she wouldn't have created as much excitement'.

Tranmere's gates rocketed as thousands of Kop-ites crossed the water to support Shankly in his new position at the little Rovers.

Derby County offered Shankly a full-time position; he assisted John Toshack at Swansea City, and Tommy Docherty was delighted to 'have the great man at Manchester United as often as possible'. Players at Old Trafford responded well to Shankly's pre-match talks, his dressing-room banter and encouragement, which Docherty also found invaluable in his management of United.

The telephone at Shankly's home in Bellefield never stopped ringing as managers and coaches constantly consulted with him, sought advice, asked an opinion of a player or just generally chatted soccer. Media relations continued with appearances on 'This Is Your Life' and 'Desert Island Discs', whilst a large audience keenly tuned into Shankly's show on Liverpool's commercial station Radio City. Radio and TV interviews, continuing his work as a visitor to Liverpool's Alder-Hey Hospital, after-dinner speaking and guest appearances at supporters clubs or local boys clubs, kept Shankly in touch with the masses. Wherever a decent match was being played, Shankly would be there; guest, of course, of the home club.

Like many other 'retired' men, Shankly, at Ness's insistence, turned his hand to gardening. This new hobby was short-lived, however, as to his wife's horror, Shankly would pull up her prize blooms thinking they were weeds. The gardening equipment was soon returned to storage.

A position scouting for Liverpool in Scotland was offered, but angrily dismissed by Shankly when he discovered that all that was really on offer was the opportunity for he and Ness to travel to Glasgow or Ayr for a few days at the club's expense. He was livid at such a patronising suggestion. How could he take club money under false pretences!

Further rifts developed between Shankly and his old club. It took Liverpool over a year and a half to invite him to away games. Liverpool were firmly distancing themselves from Shankly and really wounded him when they did get around to inviting him to a UEFA Cup final in Bruges. He was virtually ignored on the plane journey and billeted with two players' wives in an hotel some distance from the official party.

Liverpudlians marvelled at seeing this man in his sixties turning out in kick-about matches with Everton's under-14 teams. They also marvelled when Shankly, walking through the city's football parks, would discard his jacket and tie, roll up his sleeves and join in a game involving the local youths or unemployed, often dividing the lads up into Scotland versus England or Liverpool versus Everton 'teams'.

Nobody thought twice about his eccentricities, because this was the Shankly they knew and loved. He was still 'King of Anfield' as far as Merseyside was concerned, and years after his retirement there still exists resentment at how he was treated by the club.

Kevin Keegan, Shankly's greatest import, summed up the feelings of the fans: 'They named a set of gates after him but I think Liverpool should be playing in the Shankly Stadium. I think that fans would accept that. He started it off; that stadium wouldn't be what it is now if it wasn't for Bill Shankly. They might still be a club with no direction as they were when he joined. The gates are nowhere near enough and the club know that.'

Keegan, of course, refers to the Shankly gates built at Anfield in the ex-manager's honour bearing the inscription: 'You'll never walk alone.'

22

Shankly Lives Forever

During Shankly's final years, clubs with whom he was associated in the past honoured him through the construction in their stadiums of 'Shankly Suites'. He was touched when, in August 1980, Workington Town invited him back to open the club's Shankly Lounge. The postman delivering to Mr and Mrs Shankly's home in Bellefield Avenue would daily deliver a sackful of mail from supporters or well-wishers, presents from grateful Kop-ites. Shankly spent time working on his biography and discussing his life with journalists. He relaxed with his memories, especially those of the tributes paid to him by fans.

Shankly had been especially moved when, following a testimonial match held for him at Anfield in 1978, he was presented by Kop-ites with a plaque inscribed 'The Road to Glory' and a silver tankard engraved 'To Shanks, with thanks, a fan'. The rancour which had surrounded Shankly's departure sadly continued until, suddenly, on the morning of Saturday, 26 September 1981, following breakfast and a glance at the day's football fixtures in the morning paper, he suffered a heart attack and was rushed to Liverpool's Broad Green Hospital.

Liverpool was concerned on hearing the news of Shankly's

heart attack. The hospital was inundated with messages, get-well cards, flowers and calls from fans anxious to hear of Shankly's state of health. Enquiries as to his condition also came from all over Britain and Europe, every one of them anxious to show their concern.

Prayers were said. Hundreds waited outside Broad Green Hospital until finally, just after 12.30 a.m. on Tuesday, 29 September, he suffered a second and fatal heart attack.

At 1.20 a.m. the hospital released the news: 'Mr Shankly has passed away.'

Merseyside and the whole football world was stunned at the news. Shankly was dead. Throughout the city of Liverpool, grown men and women wept openly. People did not turn in for work and children were kept from school as tens of thousands of Liverpool families mourned their loss. Newspapers carried the grim banner headline: 'Shankly is Dead'. Never before, or since, has this city known such grief nor demonstrated such a public display of loss.

Flags in the city were flown at half-mast, meetings cancelled, factories, offices and shops closed as fans and admirers consoled themselves.

The pubs were quiet and the usual weekday noise of the city bustle subdued as Liverpool struggled to come to terms with the fact that the end of an era had been reached.

This had not been a good year for the city. Unemployment was rising rapidly, memories of the riots at Toxteth were still fresh – now this, the death of Shankly.

The common people knew that with Shankly's passing a good part of the vitality of their city had gone. Shankly had rallied them before in times of uncertainty and insecurity; he had united and encouraged them through past times of adversity. This wasn't just the death of a city football manager, but the passing of a father figure, a rock to whom the people had clung. It seemed as if a little part of everyone had died.

Shankly's funeral was held on Friday, 2 October 1981, at St Mary's Church in the Liverpool district of West Derby. Outside the Everton training ground at Melwood, only yards from Shankly's home, the players and staff of Everton Football Club stood in silence as Shankly's funeral cortège left Bellefield Avenue. Thousands lined the streets, heads bowed, as the solemn procession of hearse and cars passed by.

Each of England's 92 league clubs and several Scottish clubs were represented at St Mary's where great football legends such as Matt Busby, Tom Finney and dozens more looked on as Liverpool's 'six-footers', Toshack, Yeats, Hughes and Clemence, bore the coffin aloft escorted by Keegan, Callaghan and St John.

Tears were shed at the end of the church service as strains of 'You'll Never Walk Alone' filled the air. Thousands stood in silent respect as Shankly made his last journey through the streets of Liverpool to Priory Road crematorium close to Anfield stadium. Striking crematorium workers had turned out specially for the day to ensure Shankly's departure was carried out with due dignity!

Shankly has long gone from Liverpool. His legend, though, lives on forever in the hearts and minds of the Liverpudlians who so idolised the tailor's son from Glenbuck. He came in 1958, and utterly transformed the face of Liverpool FC and the football world as a whole. When will we see his like again, that flower of Scotland and freeman of Liverpool?

23

Arise Sir Bill!

Liverpool FC have never been able to divorce themselves from the late Bill Shankly, nor do they really want to, despite the bitterness of 'conspiracy theories' which surrounded his retiral. Indeed, although Kevin Keegan's suggestion that Anfield should be renamed the Shankly Stadium, as a lasting tribute to the great man's memory, has not been taken up, there are tremendous monuments to Shankly.

The impressive Shankly Gates dominate the entrance to Anfield whilst a new Anfield Museum contains artefacts of Shankly's career and a scene depicting him addressing his 'boys' in the changing-rooms before the Inter Milan game in 1965. A larger-than-life, eight-foot-tall bronze statue of Shankly in typical pose, created by celebrated Liverpool sculptor Tom Murphy, was unveiled by Ness at a ceremony outside the entrance to the Kop on 4 December 1997. This impressive monument bears the simple inscription, 'Shankly – he made the people happy'. Anfield has its Shankly Suite and the granite plinth dedicated by Liverpool (specifically by Scottish Coal and Liverpool Away Supporters Club) on the site of the now derelict Glenbuck village on 26 April 1997, will be returned to a new green-field site at the cessation of open-cast coal working in the area.

Nevertheless, the greatest tributes to the man come from

the ordinary people whom he served with honesty, compassion and integrity.

Not many outside the city of Liverpool are aware of Shankly's 'other life' which brought about the adulation he received from his fellow Liverpudlian citizens. Much has been made of the football life: his work at Anfield; the soccer successes; his relationship with the supporters. Screeds have been written or broadcast about his wit, humour and oratory skills. Liverpudlians, however, do not idolise people merely for doing their jobs. Shankly isn't still highly revered 17 years after his death simply because he was a football genius. You have to impress the people of Liverpool a lot more than that for them to accord you immortality!

Liverpudlians know who and what Shankly was as a man. He had touched so many of them personally in their own lives, meant so much more to them than politicians or civic heads, ministers or priests. His charitable acts towards thousands of fans, his unstinting efforts on behalf of causes such as the Royal National Institute for the Blind, schools for handicapped children, the disadvantaged and the sick are firmly etched in the memories of Scousers.

Shankly's interest in Alder-Hey Hospital, his continual visits to those in the city's nursing homes and hospices, holding a hand, comforting patients and relatives, never went unnoticed by the people.

When I was down in Liverpool researching this book, I wondered just how my efforts would differ from the other Shankly biographies. Shankly's record in football is well documented, so it's quite a simple task to research his life in soccer; the man's humorous quips, Shankly stories, are well enough recorded.

But reporting for *The Herald* on that windswept day at Glenbuck in April 1997, I was given a real insight into why the man was so revered in Liverpool; why Jack Moran had walked the miles from Merseyside to south Ayrshire. 'Never mind the football, Tom,' said Jack. 'Why doesn't someone tell why we really love him – why wasn't he knighted for his services to the people?'

On investigating this new angle on Shankly I set about my research in Liverpool.

Shankly's effect on people so long after his death amazed me.

On hearing that a Scots journalist was in town writing a Shankly book, Liverpudlians jammed my telephone line in Crosby for weeks, eager to recount incidents when the man had touched their lives. Many visited the house whilst several hundreds sent letters with Shankly stories. Taxi-drivers, on identifying me as the 'Shankly Book' would not charge the fare and spent their valuable time talking about Shankly.

Everywhere I went in Liverpool, people would stop me and tell their own particular Shankly story. The experience was both amazing and enlightening.

It would require another two volumes of this contribution to Shankly's memory to retell these stories, but space permits the printing of two letters concerning Shankly's work outside the football scene.

22 Larkhill
Ashurst
Skelmersdale
Lancs

Dear Mr Darby

Re Bill Shankly

In the '70s I ran a boxing club in Tower Hill, Kirkby. Each season the club would organise a large show, bringing a team from London, Ireland and so on.

On two occasions I sent off an invitation to Bill Shankly to present the cups/medals, and then one morning at 8 a.m. the telephone rang and my son Brian (aged about eight or nine and an Evertonian to boot) took the call. He then passed it to me and Bill spoke to me for a good 30 minutes, first apologising for having to refuse the invitation but saying he'd be happy to oblige another time and then asking me about myself, my wife and family, the club. This was a man whose time was at a premium yet he took the time to chat to me like an old friend. My son Brian, the only one of my six children, not a Liverpool supporter, still talks about that day.

The following year we made another request, but again he rang and regretted he couldn't make it and this time it was my wife who took the call (another Evertonian). He chatted to my wife, again about the family and society and spoke about myself, as if we were old friends. The warmth of the man and the real interest he had in people was so evident.

To think that here was the manager of Liverpool FC, the most successful team ever, ringing up personally to decline an invitation and having a friendly conversation with people he had never met is unusual to say the least. A written refusal from the club would have been acceptable and I certainly would never have expected Bill himself to take the trouble – a definite measure of the man's 'ordinariness' which only adds to his greatness!

To say Bill Shankly will never be forgotten in Liverpool is

an understatement – Bill Shankly *was* Liverpool in those days.

Yours sincerely

Patrick McElhinney

33 Mardale Lawn
Liverpool

Dear Tom

It was really good to speak to you on the phone a few days ago. I met Bill through my job, which was working in a school swimming-pool. It had been arranged for Bill to present some awards to the children after they had completed a sponsored swim.

The kids involved in the swim were (in my opinion) a bit special, because they had all suffered the awful consequences of the thalidomide sedative. Bill was impressed when he was told that the kids were swimming to raise funds for the NSPCC. The swim was not due to finish for a few hours, and Bill was waiting on the poolside when we started talking about sick children generally.

Bill told me it really upset him to come into contact with sick children. Then he spoke very emotionally of a young girl, aged 11 or 12, whom he had visited in hospital. She was very ill, suffering from cancer, and Bill told me how it had 'cut him up'. He visited the young girl a few times, and sadly she died.

Although Bill had formed a respectful closeness with the bereaved family, especially with the little one who had died, he explained to them that it would not be a good idea for him to accept their invitation to the funeral. You don't need me to tell you how much media attention Bill always attracted, and he felt this could cause added distress to the parents.

But then this lovable, hard-man character quietly said to me, 'I was at that little girl's funeral, though.' Bill found out the time and place, and he attended the cemetery, but stayed at a distance in the background. When I asked Bill if he had told the parents later what he'd done, he said, 'Nah, that's not important.' I don't know the name of the bereaved family, Tom, nor the date, but I can't help feeling they would like to have known.

There seemed to be a distant note of bitterness in Bill's voice when I mentioned his flashy Capri car outside. He sort of pointed his thumb towards it, saying something like 'that's what I've got to show for myself after finishing up with Liverpool FC'. Bill quite rightly pointed out to me the astronomical cost of the new floodlights and Kemlyn Road stand, which he had been instrumental in bringing to Anfield. Of course, he was referring not only to the huge successes on the domestic scene but also to the fantastic financial rewards from Europe. At that time (1975) I think even the Mersey Docks and Harbour Board Company were paying off their workers with more of a financial lump sum than that flashy Capri car.

Let me end on a slightly lighter note, Tom, which concerns a European game against Ajax. After being five goals down from the first leg, the headlines in the Daily Express (I think), on the day of the second leg, were 'We'll Get Seven, says Bill Shankly'. So I asked Bill (when I was talking to him on that memorable day) how the bloody hell did he get more than 40,000 people to believe him and turn up to the game?

'We would have scored seven, and won easy if Peter Thompson had not hit the bar in the sixth minute.' And, of course, I really believed him. He was the most sincere, affectionate, infectious, lovable man, that I ever had the privilege of meeting.

Sorry I'm not very articulate with the pen, Tom, but I hope you may find some aspect worth reading. Good luck with your book, and best wishes to you and your family.

Regards

Gerard Reason

There are many more such testimonials. Shankly's relationship with Liverpool fans is best described in the following letters, a selection from the many contributions by people eager to share their own particular encounter with the man.

72 Gorsewood Road
Gateacre
Liverpool

Dear Mr Darby

I note from Liverpool Echo that you are looking for stories/anecdotes regarding the late Bill Shankly. I only ever met the man once; I'm not sure about the date, it was in the early '70s just after he had resigned as Liverpool manager. No doubt if I was to do some research I would be able to find out the exact date. It was the first game of the season (at Loftus Road) and Liverpool were playing QPR. They were beaten 2–1, Gerry Francis scoring the second goal.

I had travelled down with my mates on a football special (train) and we had decided to travel back on an ordinary train – for some reason we had decided to change at Birmingham, probably because the police would have been chasing after us. We embarked on a train for Liverpool and started to work our way from the back to the front. The idea behind this was to try and find a first-class compartment that was empty. On travelling through the first-class carriages we came upon a compartment that was occupied by a single person.

This elderly man wore a grey suit, a red shirt and dark tie; he had grey hair and a warm smile, hence the man Bill Shankly. I couldn't believe it, the man I had worshipped all my life. I was the first to enter the compartment.

'Can we sit in here with you, Mr Shankly?' were the only words that came into my head.

'Sure you can, son. Have you been down to the game?' recognising that we were Scousers.

'We have,' says I.

'Sit down and tell me how they played.'

We sat in that first-class compartment and listened all the way home to Shanks talking football (in my opinion one of the most important men in the game). He told us that he had resigned so he could spend more time with Nessie, but somehow I never quite believed that, and he wasn't so convincing. He went on to hint that he did not sign Ray Kennedy, nor would he ever have done so, and I got the impression that this had been part of the problem. This being said, we spent the best couple of hours that any of us had ever had. He was absolutely fascinating. He went on to tell us that if we wanted a Saturday afternoon's entertainment we should come over to his house and sit in his front garden, and he would keep us entertained for a fee of 50p.

During our journey home we had a visit from British Transport Police who informed us that as we were illegally travelling on the train, we were to be thrown off at the next stop. Shanks piped up: 'You will not. I'll pay the fares of all these lads if I have to.'

'No need for that,' said the policeman, realising who he was talking to.

We stayed on the train and arrived at Lime Street Station, with Liverpool and their defeat well and truly forgotten. We walked down the platform with Shanks to the taxi rank.

'Anyone want a lift?'

I dived in and got a lift all the way to Shankly's house (which was miles away from mine) and I listened as Shanks entertained the taxi driver.

A couple of years later Bill Shankly died. I believe that football was his life's blood and without it he had no life. I hope this story has been of some help.

Yours sincerely

R.L. Ambrose

18 St Paul's Place
Hawthorne Road
Bootle, Merseyside

Dear Tom

I have been a supporter of Liverpool FC since 1942 and a big fan of Bill Shankly, and I witnessed the glorious things that great man did for football. I am now an OAP and can no longer afford to go to the matches. Anyway, my story of Shanks is of the day I went to renew my season ticket during the close-season of 1963.

When I arrived at Anfield on a beautiful day in early June, there was no sign of life anywhere. The ticket office was closed and everything looked dead. On investigation, I found that the door to the players' entrance was open. I went into the passage and still there was nobody there.

All of a sudden a booming voice asked me in an enchanting Scottish brogue if he could help me in any way. It was the great man himself. So, having got up off my knees, I explained that I was trying to pay my renewal money for my season ticket. He shook hands with me, took me into the office and told one of the female office staff to 'please attend to this gentleman, he is the most important person here today'.

I was overwhelmed by the man and went home on cloud nine thinking I had just spoken to God.

Good luck with your book. I will certainly buy a copy when it is published to add to my collection of Liverpool FC memorabilia.

Yours sincerely

Stanley J. Myers

26 Higher End Park
Sefton, Bootle
Merseyside

Dear Tom

Further to my telephone call on Sunday, 2 November 1997, here are some stories of Mr Shankly in the *Liverpool Echo*.

In 1966 my mother wrote to Mr Shankly sending a ten shilling note asking if he had a spare Cup final ticket for Everton versus Sheffield Wednesday for me. I am an Evertonian although my dad and mum supported Liverpool (what we called a mixed family).

Anyway, the first I knew about it was when my mum telephoned me at the station (I was a fireman) to say she had a ticket for me. Mr Shankly had sent a 70-shilling stand ticket. Believe me, I was over the moon. I had supported Everton since before the war and now at last I was going to the final. Not only that, but I would be in the stands for the first time ever.

While I was drinking in the excitement of being at Wembley I heard a voice saying, 'You must be the laddie who wanted a ticket.'

On turning I saw it was Mr Shankly together with Mr P. Robinson (Liverpool secretary) and his wife. To say I was speechless would be an understatement. There was I, a football supporter who always stood in the ground part of a stadium, sitting next to the great man himself. I could hardly believe it. During the game he talked to me, telling me about the Liverpool versus Leeds Cup final. Things still stay with me, like his criticising the white lines, him telling me to watch who's winning the 50–50 ball because that's the team that will win the game and many other things about football. I can understand how he used to say he loved the game of football as much as life itself.

I still have the programme he signed for me and also the Cup final ticket.

Many years later I came across a column of his in the *Sunday Pictorial*.

In it he wrote about the Evertonian who pestered him for a Cup final ticket (me). As usual the story was coloured a bit. I still have the newspaper clipping (I will enclose a photocopy with this letter).

I do hope you will use this story in your book as I have always wanted people to know what a wonderful, true football supporter Mr Shankly was. It would also be my grateful thanks to the man himself as I have never been able to thank him for making a dream come true, but that was just the man he was. He was one of the first managers who allied himself to the football fan who stood on the terrace, spending his money and dreams on the football terrace in hail, rain and snow, cheering on his team, whatever the colour.

Should you include this story in your book, I would be grateful if you could let me know how to get hold of a copy. Please do not hesitate to contact me should you need any further clarification.

Yours sincerely

Dennis N. Macdonald

70 Worcester Road
Bootle
Merseyside

Dear Tom

Here are a couple of facts about our Bill.

Just after he came to our club, I was working for Lyons Maid ice-cream factory as an electrician, and during the summer we used to take on extra staff to go round the streets with their ice-cream vans.

Round about this time, pro footballers' wages weren't as good as they are now, as you well know, and they didn't get much of a summer wage. So, amongst the men we took on were a few of Bill's players, mainly in the reserves. One of them, whose name I forget, said to a few of our lads: 'That man is mad – he tells us to have a boiled egg in the morning and dribble it round the plate until we get it into the eggcup.' In other words, think football all the time and never forget it.

It turned out, Tom, that he wasn't so mad after all.

He was definitely a working man's manager. Before one of our Wembley finals, a gang of building fellows went to Anfield to scrounge some tickets. As he got out of his car, after an early-morning training session, he noticed this motley collection of brickies and immediately called them into the office, which they did gladly. He opened the drawers of his desk and gave them a bundle with the words 'Gie the driver a couple as weel' (like my Scots?). By the way, I never got one.

All the best with your book, Tom, I'll look out for it when it comes out.

I played with Scotch internationals in the Middle East just after the war ended: Stan McLaren PNE, wee Willie Redpath, one called McMenemy who was a flight-lieutenant, and Harry Johnson, the Blackpool captain.

All the best

Reg Garnett

63 The Channel
Burbo Way
Wallasey
Merseyside

Dear Tom

I am writing in two capacities. Firstly, as the sports presenter for Royal 945AM based at Royal Liverpool Hospital and, secondly, as a Liverpool supporter of 40 years standing with some information for your book about Bill Shankly.

In 1978 whilst working as a probation officer in Liverpool. I was responsible for organising a five-a-side competition for young lads on probation throughout Merseyside. We wanted a sports personality to present the trophy to the winning team and it was decided that I approach Bill Shankly.

The problem was how to locate him: he had retired as manager of Liverpool and I only knew that he lived opposite Everton's training ground at Bellefield. A colleague and I visited the small cul-de-sac that was there. There were about 12 semi-detached houses and we immediately noticed there was only one painted red and white. That's the one, we thought, and proceeded to knock at the door. The lady who answered, however, informed us that Mr Shankly lived next door but one!

As it happened, Bill was at home and asked us in. I was in seventh heaven as he regaled us with stories of the Reds, particularly my heroes St John, Yeats, Hunt and Peter Thompson. I soon discovered you did not have a conversation with Bill, you listened. Whilst I was riveted my colleague, who had no interest whatsoever in football, was no doubt wondering when I was going to get around to asking him to present the medals at the final.

After an hour or so, Shanks turned to my colleague and said, 'You don't say a lot, son, but you were a bloody good wrestler. You're the Green Flash, aren't you?' It turned out that my colleague had been a wrestler in his younger years, known as the Green Flash, and had appeared on TV regularly in the early 1960s. Shanks was a keen wrestling fan and remembered him. My colleague had never revealed this in the office so from then on, needless to say, he was known as the Green Flash and took some good-natured stick!

Incidentally, Bill gladly accepted the invitation to attend the five-a-side final. He stayed for a long time after the match, signing autographs, talking to the lads and giving each a memento. Although it was offered, he adamantly refused to take any expenses. What a man!

Best wishes

Ray O'Brien

21 Dee Close
Simonswood
Kirkby, Liverpool

Dear Mr Darby,

I am writing on behalf of your request in the *Liverpool Echo* for true stories about the great gentleman Bill Shankly.

My father, having no sons, took both my sister Christine and myself to watch Liverpool FC at a very early age. Needless to say we both loved the Reds and still do. In fact, when I started courting my husband and introduced him to my dad, the first thing my dad said to him was 'Are you a Kopite, or one of *them*?' (meaning an Evertonian). Fortunately for us, he was a Red.

When my sister's 21st birthday arrived I decided to go to Anfield and have a birthday card signed by all the players. I took my two sons in their pram, one aged three months and the other three years old, as I was going to walk up from Scotland Road where I lived. When I arrived at Anfield I saw Ray Clemence going into the players' entrance so I asked him if he would ask the Liverpool players to sign the birthday card for me, which he did. After a while, Ray gave me the card back and told me that he did not get the boss's signature but he would be coming out soon. As I was talking to my three-year-old son, I turned round and saw that Bill Shankly and Bob Paisley had got into the car and started the engine. I ran over to their car and knocked on the window. Now, they need not have stopped or taken any notice of me, but they did. Mr Shankly wound down his window and asked me in his broad Scottish accent what he could do for me. I told him about the birthday card, which he immediately signed. Then he asked if there was anything else that I needed. I said I would like a request played at the match, so he got out of the car and went into the office to tell them the request himself. When he came back out he said, 'It's all done, lass', and he bent down, spoke to my two sons and ruffled their hair. He then got back into his car and waved to us as he drove away. There were no airs and graces with him and he always found time for the fans. Is it any wonder we all loved and respected him.

I hope this helps you in some way with your research, Tom, and I wish you good luck with your work.

Yours sincerely

Alice Fearns

11a Burford Avenue
Wallasey
Wirral

Dear Mr Darby

Having just read in the *Liverpool Echo* that you are looking for stories relating to the legendary Bill Shankly, I hope the following will be of interest (and useful) to you.

I can't remember the exact year – sometime in the '70s I think – Liverpool were due to play in the FA Cup final at Wembley and my friend's 20-year-old son, Billy, a staunch supporter of the Reds and a regular at Anfield, just couldn't get a ticket. Although an Evertonian myself, I decided to write to Bill and relate the story of Billy's plight – never really expecting any response. You can imagine my surprise and delight when I received a valued Wembley ticket, together with a compliment slip upon which Bill had put 'hush-hush'. Obviously, Billy was astounded that an Evertonian had managed to get such a 'gem' – but it was some years after Bill's death before I disclosed my little secret!

Best of luck with your book – I'd be grateful if you let me know when it is published.

Yours sincerely

Lilian G. Smith

2 Ranworth Place
Norris Green
Liverpool

Dear Tom

I write concerning your article in the *Liverpool Echo* requesting information on the great Bill Shankly.

As you might know, Tom, Liverpool had a dismal record before Bill Shankly took over as manager. In the 1953–54 season Liverpool played 42 matches, won nine, drew ten, lost 23; goals for 68; goals against 97; points 28. Five or six years later, after being on the verge of promotion every season, Liverpool board directors appointed Bill Shankly as manager. In his second full season at Anfield, he took Liverpool back into the First Division. They had won eight points clear of Leyton Orient. After that, the rest is history. Liverpool had a fantastic run of success under Bill Shankly: they won the league championship twice, 1963–64 and '65–'66; and in 1965 won the FA Cup for the first time in their history, beating Leeds United. After that came Europe and the Cup-Winners final in 1966, beating Juventus, Standard Liege, Honved Hungary and the mighty Celtic in the semi-final. Liverpool went on to play Borussia Dortmund of West Germany in the final at Hampden Park, Borussia beating Liverpool 2–1. It was a sad day for Bill Shankly and all the fans who had made the journey north. But Shankly bounced back and took Liverpool to greater heights.

Bill only ever talked about Liverpool football team, never mentioning their rivals Everton. When someone asked him about the two great teams in Liverpool, he said yes, there are two great teams: Liverpool and Liverpool Reserves. He once said of Liverpool FC: 'At Anfield we train together, eat together, we also sit in the lounge and talk football together. In fact, this club is a family.'

The Kop in Liverpool's ground always sang his praises. Liverpool would not be the great club they are today were it not for Bill Shankly. We had 14 years of that hero, until his retirement in 1974, but he left behind a team that went on to higher things.

Bill Shankly was also a very funny man. He was once asked where he took his wife for their anniversary, to which he replied: 'Of course I didn't take my wife to see Rochdale as an anniversary present, it was her birthday. Would I have got married during the football season? And anyway, it wasn't Rochdale, it was Rochdale reserves.'

A reporter once questioned Shankly about the fact that one of Liverpool's finest players, Roger Hunt, had missed a few easy goals at a home match. He replied: 'Yes, he misses a few. But he gets in the right place to miss them.' During the referees' clampdown in 1971, he said the trouble with referees is that 'they know the rules but they don't know the game'.

In 1972, when Liverpool, Derby County and Manchester City were chasing the championship, Shankly said to Joe Mercer before Derby versus City: 'I hope you both lose.' He also said, 'I'm a people's man, a players' man. You could call me a humanist.' But I think one of the best quotes from Bill Shankly was when he said, 'Football is not a matter of life and death, it's much more important than that.'

I hope this is of some help to you, Tom. Good luck with your book.

P.C. Ball

Old Swan Fire Station
Liverpool

Dear Tom

Before I was old enough to go to the match at Anfield with my brothers and cousins, I used to play football on the grass verge outside our house, watch the final scores on television, then run out and play more football and wait for Bill Shankly to drive past on his way home to West Derby, and give him a wave. This happened for a few years, and he always returned it with a smile and a wave.

When I was approximately eight years old, my brothers agreed to take me to my first ever match. It was Liverpool versus Coventry 1973. We were in the 'boys' pen' but halfway through the second half we walked through into the Kop. We couldn't see a thing, but we didn't mind. We won and we were in the mighty Kop.

When the final whistle went, everybody just turned in an instant and headed for the exits. Since I didn't expect it, I was swept away with the crowds. All that I could see were jeans pockets with rolled up programmes, shoes and bums. I was then taken down stairways, along passageways and out into the street. I did not have a clue where I was, where my brothers were, or in which direction to walk home. I walked around the stadium, hoping to meet someone, but to no avail. I was well and truly lost and beginning to get anxious and upset. Just then I thought about Bill Shankly knowing the way to my home. I knew that I could trust him to show me the right way to go. So I went to the main reception and waited. When Bill came out, he was with his brother and they were both wearing white raincoats.

After autograph hunters and well-wishing fans had left, I walked up to him and said 'Excuse me, Bill', and told him my predicament. I thought he would give me directions, but when he opened the door to his beige-coloured Mark 1 Capri, pulled the seat forward and said, 'Climb in', I could hardly believe it. I knew then that I was safe and that I would be okay.

As we pulled out of the Shankly Gates he just said, 'Shout out when we get there, son.'

As we drove down Pinehurst Avenue, I told him that I lived in Lisburn Lane, to which he replied, 'Are you the little man who's always playing football and gives me a wave?'

'Yes,' I said, 'that's me.' And the three of us laughed together. I was amazed that he had remembered.

When we got to Lisburn Lane, we drove up to our house and my brothers, mates and cousins were, as ever, playing football outside on the grass verge.

They ran up, waving and calling to Bill Shankly, but when I climbed out of the back seat, shouting, 'Thanks, Bill', the others stopped dead in amazement. They couldn't believe their eyes. We all ran into the house to tell my mum that I was home safely thanks to Bill Shankly.

A Fireman

37 Durham Road
Seaforth
Liverpool

Dear Mr Darby

I read with interest your appeal in last Friday's *Liverpool Echo* for any stories, anecdotes, etc. about Bill Shankly, and I thought you may be interested in the following story.

Not long after Bill retired from-managing Liverpool FC, a book was published called *Bill Shankly – A Legend in his Own Lifetime*. It was a limited edition and my mother, Norah Blackburn – a fanatical Liverpool FC supporter – managed to purchase a copy. The book contained pages of tributes from the Liverpool players of the day, the backroom staff, and also local celebrities of the time. At the bottom of each page of the person's tribute was a box for an autograph. Over a period of time, my mum managed to get all the footballers to sign on the appropriate page – she even managed to get John Smith (Liverpool FC's chairman) to sign it. Eventually, all the autographs were collected. However, my mum wasn't satisfied and decided that, in order to make the book complete, Bill Shankly should sign the front page. Therefore she wrote to Bill (everyone in Liverpool knew he lived in Bellefield Avenue – the joke was that it was his means of 'spying on the opposition' – it was Everton FC's training ground!). She said she'd meet him 'anytime, anywhere', and awaited his reply.

Bill phoned a couple of times and said that he'd come to our house, but wasn't sure exactly where we were, so he was looking into it. Anyway (and luckily for me), I was on half-term from school and the phone rang. I answered it and heard the unmistakable voice on the other end: 'Is that Norah?'

'No,' I replied, 'it's her daughter, Sheila.'

'Oh,' Bill said. 'It's Bill Shankly here . . . can you tell your mum that I'll be down to see her in half an hour or so.' He said goodbye and hung up.

You should have seen my mum and I panic! We'd been in

the middle of cleaning the house and suddenly had to put everything back into place, and make ourselves look respectable in half an hour! We managed to gain some semblance of order, and when the doorbell rang I opened the door. Bill walked in and gave me a big hug and a kiss on the cheek, and greeted my mum in the same way . . . it felt more like we were meeting with a relative, or old friend, rather than with someone we had never met before.

Bill came in and sat down and chatted with us for about an hour and a half. He signed my mum's book with a red felt pen, and also signed a photo for me. He was absolutely amazing to talk to . . . he told us what Anfield was like when he first arrived and related the ins and outs of Liverpool's matches from years earlier with the most minuscule of details – even down to the size of the crowd.

All too quickly he had to leave, but not before my mum took a photo of him in our front room, and with me sitting on the arm of the chair.

The memory of this occasion has stayed with me from that day in 1977, and even now it is my 'claim to fame' to tell of the day Bill Shankly came to our house for tea and biscuits. Even 20 years later, people are still fascinated by my story . . . some even ask if they can touch my hand because I've met Bill Shankly . . . such is the unending love and admiration people have for him.

If you would like a copy of the photo of Bill and me, I could send you one. In the same way, if you would like any further details about Bill's visit, don't hesitate to contact me. My mother died earlier this year, so I'm relating this story on her behalf because, without her doing what she did, I would not be able to tell people about the day I met Bill Shankly.

I hope you can use this story in your book. Either way, I would be very interested to read your book, and would like to wish you ever success in its development and publication.

Yours sincerely

S.J. Robinson (Mrs)

417 Storrington Heys
Storrington Avenue
Croxteth
Liverpool

Hi Tom

Ron the Scouser here. Hope you got my previous letter. The reason I never put my home address on my letter was because certain members of my family who are Evertonians would have been 'extracting the urine' – and being Blues, they have got to be 'basket cases'. You must agree?! However, if you wish to write to me, use the address above, of my pal Rob Jones (no, not the Liverpool defender, Tom).

Just a couple more 'Shanklyisms' to tell you now!

Liverpool were at home, playing a top team. A journalist said to Shanks: 'I was talking to their manager – he said he was confident of getting a good result here today – what do you think?'

Shanks growled, 'The only thing he'll get at Anfield is a cup of tea at half-time!'

Journalists loved interviewing Shanks for his dry, quick-fire wit and home-spun philosophy – which reminds me of an occasion when he was being interviewed, in front of the empty Kop terraces. The interviewer said, 'I've heard that, in this city, football is a kind of religion – a matter of life or death, so to speak?'

Shanks replied: 'Oh no, laddie – it's much more serious than that!'

He was sometimes referred to as 'a Scottish James Cagney'. I can imagine him, at the height of his fame, standing with arms outstretched on the roof of the Kop shouting, 'I'm on top of the world, Ma!' (I suppose you've seen that Cagney film?).

Well, Tom, I've enjoyed writing to you. Once again I apologise for my writing, due to my arthritis. I hope your stay in Liverpool is an enjoyable one for you. Before I finish, here are a couple of teasers to try on your friends, okay? Right –

which famous Liverpool player was always picked by England but never wore an England shirt in his career? Answer – Ian Rush. He was always picked by Mike England to play for Wales!

Two Scousers in a pub, neither of them wearing scarves or football shirts: how do you know which one of them supports Liverpool? He's the one with a slight cockney accent!

I'll sign off now, Tom, hoping that your book is a monumental success – it will be here in Liverpool! God bless you and those you love.

Ron (The Kopite)

4 Balmoral Road
Liverpool

Dear Tom

As requested, just a few words about our first experience of Bill Shankly's tremendous charisma.

After 73 years of trying, Liverpool FC had finally won the FA Cup under the leadership of the inspirational Bill Shankly.

I had been to the game on the Saturday with a gang of mates and had celebrated the famous victory in London, catching the last train home from the capital. I arrived home at 8 a.m. to find my eight-year-old daughter sat up in bed. She was overcome with excitement, describing to me how her mother had rushed home from work to tell her that Liverpool had won the Cup.

No further sleep was to be had that morning as we prepared for our visit to the town centre to welcome our heroes back home with the FA Cup.

We arrived at the Town Hall with great excitement. We were two hours early, which was just as well because within half an hour you could hardly see an empty space, including the tops and sides of the buildings. There must have been 750,000 people in the city.

When the team and staff arrived, accompanied by the Lord Mayor and civic dignitaries, and appeared on the Town Hall balcony, the small figure of Shanks was barely visible. However, after several fruitless attempts to make themselves heard above the incredible noise (somebody said it was louder than when the bombs were falling in the May Blitz 1940), the small compact figure of Bill Shankly moved towards the mike.

As he approached the instrument the din rose to a crescendo. The 'Messiah' was about to speak. Personally, I thought it would be impossible to hear a word. I was mistaken. I had not until then been aware of the sheer magnetism and power of the man's personality. As that figure, dwarfed by the building and immense crowd, raised his arms, the crowd fell silent. Not a sound could be heard until that fine, powerful voice boomed out with its vibrant Ayrshire accent, 'We are the greatest team in the world.' He paused to allow the wall of noise rise like a tidal wave. The roar continued for what seemed an age. Then once again the raised arms demanded, and got, complete silence and rapt attention. He continued. 'And you are the greatest supporters in the world.' The noise that followed that short sentence was impossibly louder than ever.

Witnessing these scenes and the effect that Shankly's presence had on the crowd made my spine tingle and my hair stand up. Thousands of Liverpudlians were convinced that he was football's saviour.

I hope this little story helps you, Tom. I'll be asking some of my friends about their particular stories and I'll pass them on to you. In the meantime if there is anything I can do to help, don't hesitate to give me a ring.

Yours sincerely

Peter Crook

Others tell of occasions when Shankly stepped into their lives at times of crisis.

Jack Moran said: 'He helped youngsters start off in life, pestered the council over people's housing problems, and if he heard of a particular situation giving a fan's family grief, he'd step in to help.' Jack, like so many others, still has a photograph of Bill Shankly in his living-room.

Shankly kissed babies and shook thousands of hands. Not, however, in the way an aspiring politician would at the hustings. His was a warm handshake, the gentle kiss placed on the forehead of a child was meant as a gesture of love, the love he had in his heart for the people of Liverpool who had welcomed himself, Ness and the family into their hearts, their homes.

The lad from Glenbuck had become a Liverpudlian, proud that his grandchildren 'were growing up with good Scouse accents'.

There can be no doubt that Shankly was a socialist. 'I am a socialist naturally because I am a coalminer.' Though never a student or reader of politics, he was a 'gut socialist' in the old south Ayrshire tradition. Socialism to Shankly was akin to Christianity in the true sense. He would often say: 'Jesus Christ was the first socialist!' His own particular brand of politics was about compassion, honesty, caring for your fellow, the spirit of community. The socialism of Glenbuck!

Shankly's working-class brand of socialism had its roots in the old Independent Labour Party of Keir Hardie and Jenny Lee. A Labour hero was Nye Bevan. He well knew the meaning of the word capitalism and though he never moved to communism, he had a lifelong distrust of financial whizzkids or entrepreneurs. Shankly was more at home with the common people – his 'ain folk'. Football to Shankly was 'socialism in action', discipline, hard work, teamwork – just rewards at the end of the day. His footballers, like the fans, were the workers. There is little doubt in the minds of Scousers that Shankly was never considered for a knighthood because of his outspoken distrust of politicians, his having no use for royalty and his unswerving allegiance to the people.

It's true he never won the European Cup whilst Sir Jock Stein and Sir Matt Busby did. But surely, argue the citizens of Liverpool, he achieved much more in his time at Liverpool than his two Scottish contemporaries did at Celtic Park and Old Trafford?

Stein's Celtic won league titles in ten successive years but would they would have achieved this in the English League? And if winning the European Cup means an automatic knighthood, why haven't a few more been handed out to English managers in recent years? People are knighted for their services to industry. Wasn't Liverpool an industry, argue the Kop-ites?

As Britain enters the new millennium with all the planned celebrations of past glories which are to take place, would it not be a fitting compliment to Shankly and the people of Liverpool if part of those celebrations included a celebration of the life and times of a lad from Glenbuck, a genius, a legend in his own lifetime who dedicated that life's work 'to making the people happy'?

Shanks for the memories!

24

The Shankly Quips

Shankly's quick wit, his Ayrshire humour and naïvety are, like the man himself, legendary. Some of the Shankly stories have been exaggerated, some change as the years pass. If the final pages of Shankly's story were a bit depressing, then the following selection of Shankly quotes should correct the imbalance.

Everton Stories

Following Everton's defeat in the 1971 Cup semi-final, Shankly is reputed to have quipped: 'Sickness would not have kept me away from this one. If I'd been dead I'd have had them bring my coffin to the ground, prop it up in the stand and cut a hole in the lid.'

'There's only two teams in Liverpool – Liverpool and Liverpool Reserves!'

At the funeral of legendary Everton star Dixie Dean, Shankly observed: 'Now whilst this is a sad occasion, I think Dixie would have been amazed to know that even in death he could draw a bigger crowd than Everton do on a Saturday afternoon.'

On awaiting Everton's arrival for a derby game at Anfield, Shankly is said to have given a box of toilet rolls to the Liverpool doorman saying: 'Give them these when they arrive – they'll need them.'

'I always look in the Sunday paper to see where Everton are in the league – starting, of course, from the bottom up.'

'The difference between Everton and the Queen Mary is that Everton carry more passengers.'

One foreign journalist covering a European tie over at Anfield asked Shankly if, with his complimentary lunch, he could merely have a big selection of vegetables. Shankly immediately told the man how to get to Goodison, saying: 'You'll find the biggest selection of vegetables in Liverpool down there.'

In General

On taking his players backstage at the London Palladium to meet Tommy Cooper, he noticed the comic magician's size 13 shoes. 'Christ, son, what size are they? I've sailed to Ireland in smaller boats!'

'It's great grass at Anfield – professional grass.'

On failing to sign Lou Macari from Celtic: 'He couldn't play anyway – I only wanted him for the reserves.'

'The trouble with you, son, is that all your brains are in your head.'

During a five-a-side match at Melwood, Shankly scored a goal which the others insisted was offside. He turned to Chris Lawler, the quietest lad in the squad, asking: 'Was it a goal? Was I offside?'
   'You were, Boss,' replied a nervous Lawler.

'Christ, son, you've been here four years, hardly said a word and, when you do, it's a bloody lie.'

'With Ron Yeats in defence we could play Arthur Askey in goal.'

And What They Said About Shankly

Canon Arnold Myers at Shankly's funeral: 'Bill Shankly did not live for himself but for a team, a vast family, for a city, for an ideal.'

Gerry Marsden at the 1997 Mersey Marvel Awards in the Moat House Hotel: 'Good luck with the book: you're writing about one of the greatest people the world has known.'

Tom Finney: 'Shankly was a model, a man to look up to.'

Ron Yeats at Glenbuck: 'He was the greatest person I know.'

Kevin Keegan: 'I always carry a picture of him, he comes into my conversation a lot; I learned a lot from him and owe the man a great deal.'

Alex Young, following a match between a Liverpool Scots XI and Liverpool English XI when Shankly managed the Scots: 'Bill Shankly was the greatest manager. I really admired him and would have loved to have played under him.'

Brian Clough: 'He's broken the silly myth that nice guys don't win anything.'

Jack Moran: 'Shankly was a genius and needs to be remembered. There will never be another like him in football.'

Brian Hall: 'Shankly was immense – a one-off.'

BBC Radio Merseyside sports commentator Alan Jackson

tells of the time when as a young DJ and announcer at Anfield he was sitting in his announcer's cubby-hole one match day when Shankly burst in saying: 'Jesus Christ, son, can ye no' talk into that microphone when the players are in the penalty box. You're putting them off, you're doing more damage than the opposition.'

The stories are plentiful but the final epitaph goes to Tommy Solomon who tells the story: 'Shankly and two players went into the chip shop across the road from Anfield after winning the FA Cup, having changed into their blazers for parading the Cup to the city centre. Shankly was ordering up a fish supper for each of the players when a woman asked: 'Mr Shankly, shouldn't they be having steak suppers?'

'No, lass,' replied Shankly. 'They'll get steak suppers when they win the double!'

25

Shankly's Football Record

Career as a player:
Cronberry Juniors 1930–32
Carlisle United July 1932–July 1933
Preston North End July 1933–March 1949

Wartime clubs as a guest player:
Norwich, Preston North End, Liverpool, Arsenal, Luton Town, Bolton Wanderers, East Fife, Partick Thistle.

International Caps for Scotland:
1938 v England
1939 v England
1939 v Wales
1939 v Northern Ireland
1939 v Hungary
Plus wartime international caps in friendlies and 'aid matches'.

Managerial achievements:

CARLISLE

Joined March 1949, first game in charge 9 April

Season	Played	Won	Drew	Lost	Final League Position
1948–49	7	1	4	2	15th Division 3 North
1949–50	42	16	15	11	9th Division 3 North
1950–51	46	25	12	9	3rd Division 3 North

GRIMSBY

Joined July 1951

Season	Played	Won	Drew	Lost	Final League Position
1951–52	46	29	8	9	2nd Division 3 North
1952–53	46	22	9	15	5th Division 3 North
1943–54*	26	11	4	11	17th Division 3 North

* Shankly resigned on 2 January 1954

WORKINGTON

Became manager 6 January 1954

Season	Played	Won	Drew	Lost	Final League Position
1953–54	20	8	6	6	18th Division 3 North
1954–55	46	18	14	1	48th Division 3 North
1955-56*	19	9	3	7	

* Shankly resigned on 15 November 1955

HUDDERSFIELD

Joined 10 December 1955, became manager 5 November 1956

Season	Played	Won	Drew	Lost	Final League Position
1956–57	26	11	4	11	12th Division 2
1957–58	42	14	16	12	9th Division 2
1958–59	42	16	8	18	14th Division 2
1959–60*	19	8	5	5	6th Division 2

* Shankly resigned on 1 December 1959

LIVERPOOL

Joined December 1959, first game in charge 19 December

Season	Played	Won	Drew	Lost	Final	League Position
1959–60	21	11	5	5	3rd	Division 2
1960–61	42	21	10	11	3rd	Division 2
1961–62	42	27	8	7	1st	Division 2
1962–63	42	17	10	15	8th	Division 1
1963–64	42	26	5	11	1st	Division 1
1964–65	42	17	10	15	7th	Division 1
1965–66	42	26	9	7	1st	Division 1
1966–67	42	19	13	10	5th	Division 1
1967–68	42	22	11	9	3rd	Division 1
1968–69	42	25	11	6	2nd	Division 1
1969–70	42	20	11	11	5th	Division 1
1970–71	42	17	17	8	5th	Division 1
1971–72	42	24	9	9	3rd	Division 1
1972–73	42	25	10	7	1st	Division 1
1973–74	42	22	13	7	2nd	Division 1

HONOURS AS LIVERPOOL MANAGER

1961–62	Champions	Division Two
1962–63	FA Cup	semi-finalists
1963–64	Champions	Division One
1964–65	FA Cup winners	European Cup semi-finalists
1965–66	Champions	Division One
	European Cup-Winners Cup runners-up	
1970–71	FA Cup runners-up	European Cup-Winners Cup semi-finalists
1972–73	Champions	Division One
	UEFA Cup winners	Manager of the Year trophy
1973–74	FA Cup winners	

26

Make the People Happy: The Shankly Statue

Hundreds of Liverpudlians assembled outside the entrance to Anfield's Kop end on Thursday, 4 December 1997, to witness the unveiling of a permanent tribute to Bill Shankly. On that date, Liverpool FC and sponsors Carlsberg hosted a ceremony at Anfield to open the newly constructed Anfield Museum of Football History, containing memorabilia depicting the club's 109-year history, and to display, yet again, Liverpool FC's undying gratitude to Bill Shankly through the erection of an incredibly lifelike bronze statue of the great man in typical pose.

The statue, commissioned by Carlsberg, was created by Liverpool sculptor Tom Murphy. Tom worked with Carlsberg's design consultants, Lawson Marshall Cole, who co-ordinated the project to establish the style and attitude of the three-quarter-ton bronze which stands on a four-sided plinth fashioned appropriately from Scottish granite, recalling Shankly's days as an Ayrshire coal miner.

Standing outside the Anfield visitor centre and new museum under the Kop, the statue is discreetly illuminated during the hours of darkness and stands as a permanent reminder of Shankly's considerable achievements at Liverpool FC.

Sculptor Tom used film, photographic and biographical references in order to capture the dynamism and spirit of Shankly, producing an outstanding piece of uncanny, lifelike work.

The Shankly statue proudly salutes the Kop showing the legendary figure in a typical posture, arms outstretched, fists clenched and wearing a supporter's scarf.

It bears the simple legend: 'He made the people happy.'

Following the statue's unveiling by Ness Shankly, former Liverpool players and invited guests from the football world mingled with the hundreds of fans who assembled to view the unveiling. Flowers were laid at the statue base, hundreds posed for photographs 'beside Shankly' and tributes were paid to the man whose statue is saluted by the thousands who make their way into the Kop on match day whispering, as they pass, 'Hello, Bill. It's good to see you.'

27

Walk On, Walk On . . . Jack Moran's Walk to Glenbuck

Lone Ayrshire piper, William Graham, silenced the noisy supporters of Liverpool and Manchester United during a clash of the Reds at Anfield stadium on Saturday, 19 April 1997. Nearly 50,000 fans who had filled Anfield to witness that afternoon's Premiership match stood in complete silence as the kilted Scots piper led pensioner Jack Moran onto the Anfield pitch at half-time to salute the Kop before setting off on a marathon 230-mile walk from Liverpool to Bill Shankly's birthplace in Glenbuck.

Jack, a 67-year-old fitness fanatic from Endbutt Lane, Crosby, was setting out on a solo sponsored walk which was to end with his arrival at Glenbuck one week later on 26 April, when legions of Liverpool fans would gather on the desolate Ayrshire moorland to dedicate the Shankly Memorial Plinth.

The fierce rivalry was halted for a time as both Liverpool and United stood in respectful silence as the pipes played Shankly's favourite hymn, 'Amazing Grace'. Tears flowed as Kop-ites waved Jack off on his walk accompanied by the strains of 'You'll Never Walk Alone'.

Jack's walk was to raise over £12,000 in sponsorship for Father Francis O'Leary's St Joseph's Cancer Hospice in Liverpool. En route to Glenbuck, Jack called in at Preston North End and Carlisle United Football Clubs – two of Shankly's former teams where he served both as player and manager – before continuing his trek through Dumfries and Galloway and the south Ayrshire hills to Glenbuck.

At the conclusion of his week-long trek, Jack was welcomed into the derelict site of what had formerly been Shankly's birthplace by several hundred Liverpool fans, guests and dignitaries who had assembled to dedicate the memorial plinth donated to South Ayrshire Council by Scottish Coal and Liverpool Away Supporters Club.

Jack joined the crowd of supporters as they huddled round the monument, a large oblong granite plinth – black to represent the gleaming Ayrshire coal, and with gold lettering bearing the words:

'Seldom in the history of sport can a village the size of Glenbuck have produced so many who reached the pinnacle of achievement in their chosen sport. This monument is dedicated to their memory and to the memory of one man in particular, Bill Shankly – **The legend, the genius, the man.**'

Source: *Plinth*

Following the monument's dedication by Ron Yeats and the Provost of South Ayrshire council, the Liverpool Red Army, who had travelled to the desolate Ayrshire moorland site of Glenbuck by coaches and cars, sang 'Amazing Grace' once more to the accompaniment of Piper Graham.

Emotions welled up as the Liverpudlians spontaneously burst into the verses of 'You'll Never Walk Alone', then filled the moorland for a whole quarter of an hour with the sound of 'Shankly! – Shankly! – Shankly! – Shankly!' to the tune of 'Amazing Grace'.

Following the dedication, Liverpool fans began lifting lumps of turf from the site of the former village, mimicking Scotland supporters who had similarly taken Wembley turf following a famous Scotland victory over England some years earlier.

Fans were taking home a piece of Glenbuck to plant in their own little gardens or allotments in the various districts of Liverpool.

To close the day's proceedings a youth football match was held, involving youngsters from the Shankly Reds and the Junior Cherrypickers. They were competing for the Bill Shankly Cup, a trophy specially donated for the occasion by Liverpool Away Supporters Club.

As the Liverpool army which had come to pay tribute to the memory of Shankly made its way homeward that memorable evening, Jack Moran said: 'I've walked these miles out of respect for Bill Shankly and to raise money for a much needed cause. Bill would have appreciated that more than anything. He was a great man and is dearly loved today in Liverpool. I'd walk a million miles for Shankly.'

'Yea, and you wouldn't be alone, mate!' said Kevin from Bootle, proudly clutching his sod of Glenbuck turf. 'This goes where it belongs, in my back garden as a permanent reminder of the everlasting bond between that little spot and Scotland and Liverpool.'

Glenbuck has gone, devoured into an open-cast coal operation on the south Ayrshire moorland. However, in the new millennium, Scottish Coal will landscape the area at the cessation of open-cast workings and resite the Shankly plinth – which is presently in storage – on the spot which was once Glenbuck.

When that happens, said Jack Moran, 'I'll walk back again just to say "Hello Bill!"'

Epilogue

Remember Glenbuck

The glen is silent now, no one would know
that here, where gorse and thistles grow,
a thousand people lived with pride
until the village died.

A store stood in that clump of birch
and there's the shadow of a church,
the school lies scattered on the ground,
it's now a rubble mound.

But see that patch of moorland fern,
down there where sheep graze by the burn,
beneath that wilderness concealed,
you'll find a football field.

Go down and walk upon that land
for that was once a hallowed stand,
out here they shaped the people's game,
a field of dreams, a place of fame.

They crawled in darkness underground
until they heard the whistle sound,
then left the danger and the dark
to run in sunlight on that park.

EPILOGUE

Their team was forged from guts and coal,
it captured Glenbuck's heart and soul,
now miners fought for village glory
to write the Cherrypickers' story.

They played with style, they beat the rest,
those Cherrypickers were the best,
wealthy clubs came for the men
who had the magic of the Glen.

But fate holds cards of joy and sorrow,
we live today, depart tomorrow.
She dealt her hand – the story ended,
and broken dreams cannot be mended.

The pit was closed, it didn't pay
and closure took all work away,
that one decision, it was said,
killed Glenbuck dead.

A ruined Glen, a flooded mine,
a boy who lost his chance to shine
but in his heart he vowed one day
to win the Cherrypickers' way.

His name was Shankly, he was the best,
his memory shines above the rest.
He won the heart of every fan,
he dignified the working man.

He came to Liverpool, he built a team,
he brought alive his Glenbuck dream,
and Anfield, his adopted home,
made sure he never walked alone.

Don Gillespie

Whispers

O, could the Glenbuck Burn but speak,
An' tales of yore unfauld –
But hark! dae I hear whispers
Frae its waters clear an' cauld?

Listen – just listen tae its chatter
As it gurgles ower the stanes;
It's tellin' noo o' fitba lads,
O' Knoxes, Taits and Bains.

O' lads frae Vass's Buildin's,
Grasshill an' Monkey Raw,
O' some o' the best auld players
That ever kicked a ba'.

It whispers names o' bygone days,
Wha played upon its banks,
Wha syne won fame an' glory
An' reached the highest ranks.

An' as it murmurs softly on,
It naither fights nor bickers,
It kens tham a', an' tells the tale
O' the Glenbuck Cherrypickers.

O' could we but its story print,
Glenbuck would hae nae fears
That the memory o' the 'Cherries'
Wad fade wi' passin' years.

Wi' our brief efforts we ha'e tried
Tae keep their names alive,
An' trust that in life's pathways
Their glories will survive.

William Tweedie

Acknowledgements

The author would like to express his eternal gratitude to all those who assisted with the research of this book and to those who helped with its publication.

Thanks to Ness Shankly and her niece Barbara, Liverpool FC, Everton FC, Jack Moran, Brian Hall, Ron Yeats, Jimmy Flowers, Tommy Solomon and all at The Albert, John Moran, Gerry Marsden, Martin, Cybil and the Taylor family, Ray O'Brien, Alan Jackson, Roger Philips and all at BBC Radio Merseyside, Tony Martin, Jim Bertram, Blyth Mitchell, Carl, Ruth and the Paul family, my daughter Heather Darby and her family Megan, Dylan and Mikey, Liverpool City Libraries, Tom and Janet, Foxy, Colwyn, Alice and Sable, and especially Vivien who encouraged and prompted me throughout a period of uncertainty and financial hardship.

Thanks to the following for reference material: *Bill Shankly – It's Much More Important Than That*, Stephen F. Kelly; *Shanks*, Dave Bowler; *The Shankly Legend*, Bernard Hale; *Shankly*, Phil Thompson; *Tosh*, John Toshack; *The Cherrypickers*, Rev. H.M. Fauls and W. Tweedie Jr.; *Pead – Liverpool: a Complete Record*. Also to the following newspapers: The *Liverpool Echo*, *The Herald* and *The Kop*.

Thanks to Mainstream Publishing for taking the book on

and to the many, many contributors who rang me, wrote to me or discussed Shankly with me.

Most of all, a big thank you to all the Scousers I encountered during 1997 and to whom this book is dedicated.

I'll be back some day to your great city, populated by the finest folk on earth.

'Shanks for the memories.'